"A SPELLBINDING MEMOIR."
—*Library Journal*

"[Snyder] paints a vivid portrait of small-town life in the years after World War II as experienced by a young girl."
—*The Washington Post Book World*

"Exquisite . . . A rare act of empathy and compassion . . . Snyder has reached out across time to draw a heartbreaking portrait of his mother as a girl in love, and a woman brave enough to sacrifice herself for her sons."
—*Austin-American Statesman*

"A profoundly thoughtful book that cannot help but touch anyone who has lost an adored one. His writing goes right to the heart of the matter—and the heart of the reader."
—*Miami Herald*

"Compelling . . . The intensity of Snyder's emotion holds the book together. . . . [He] makes real to us his mother's young life. And in his search for her true spirit, he finds that the girl who thought herself so undeserving, in giving birth to her twin sons, may have committed the most generous act any of us can offer."
—*St. Petersburgh Times*

"Snyder offers poignant glimpses into everyday family situations, reminding us of the love present in our own lives. A bittersweet story."
—*Kirkus Reviews*

"Engrossing . . . Snyder's painstaking evocation of his emotional odyssey in search of a young woman with extraordinary courage will resonate."
—*Publishers Weekly*

"Snyder pulls us into this ferocious journey."
—*Booklist*

Of Time and Memory

Of Time and Memory

A Mother's Story

❖

DON J. SNYDER

BALLANTINE BOOKS • NEW YORK

For Jack

WINTER 1997

A Ballantine Book
Published by The Ballantine Publishing Group

www.randomhouse.com/BB/

A Library of Congress Catalog Card Number is
available upon request from the publisher.

ISBN 0-345-42769-6

Cover design by Barbara Leff
Cover photo courtesy of the author

Manufactured in the United States of America

First paperback edition: March 2001

10 9 8 7 6 5 4 3 2 1

Foreword to the Paperback Edition, May 2000

Soon after I found my way to my mother's grave, I had a dream. She was teaching me to dance. I was a very old man, and she was still young and lovely. Still just a girl. She was playing Tommy Dorsey records, and Glen Miller and I asked her if she had anything by the Beatles. She laughed and said to me, "You missed the best music. The swing music was the music of my time, and there's never been such good music again."

In my dream she was trying to teach me to jitterbug and I was taking my awkward steps while I stared at her. I just kept staring at her. I told her that she had missed all the wonderful things in my life—my marriage to Colleen, the births of our children. She let me finish, and then she took my hand and told me that she hadn't missed any of those things. She had been there beside me.

It had taken me almost fifty years to find where my mother was buried. That was the spring of 1999, when I was writing the last chapters of this book. By then I was old enough to have been her father at the age she was when she died.

The journey of this book, which ends in the Lutheran Cemetery in Hatfield, Pennsylvania, began with a photograph that my father sent me at Christmas in 1997. It was an old black-and-white picture of a bride and groom in the backseat of their honeymoon car, a picture which evoked a time just after World War II and carried with it a high sense of promise in the faces of the young husband and his beautiful bride, who wore a garland of flowers in her hair.

My father never spoke of her. Once, when I was a small boy, he told me that my mother's name was Peggy and that she was in heaven. I didn't know that she was just nineteen years old when she died, or that she lived only sixteen days after she gave birth to me and my twin brother in August of 1950.

But now my father had sent me this photograph, and after all the years of silence, we began to talk about Peggy. Or I should say, I began to ask my father questions. And when I discovered that he no longer remembered his own love story—where he had first seen Peggy, where they were when he asked her to marry him or what had caused her death—I committed myself to recovering that love story for him. Here was my intention: I would go back to my mother's hometown and find everyone still alive who had known her and my father during the eleven months they had together before her death, and I would write their love story and present it to my father as a gift to him in the last years of his life. Here was an old man who, in order to survive the terrible pain of his broken love story, had made himself forget how greatly he had been loved as a boy. But I would give all of that back to him now.

Because my mother's death was the saddest thing people in Hatfield could remember, no one had forgotten her. There were the bridesmaids and ushers from their wedding, the schoolteachers, shopkeepers and neighbors, all of them eager to share their memories with me. Some of these people had wondered for half a century what had killed this young girl and what had become of her husband and their twin babies.

It was, for me, a labor of love and the writing of this book—five hundred mornings from four A.M. until ten—was the first effortless writing I had ever done in my life. I awoke each morning to the sound of my mother's voice in my darkened room, a voice that is sewn through the sentences of this book.

What I have learned from all of this is nothing less than the mystery of love. Almost fifty years ago, my mother died when she was nineteen years old—just when she was beginning to believe in the possibilities of love. She gave birth to me and my twin brother, and sixteen days later she was dead. I knew her for only sixteen days. But this is the exquisite nature of love's mystery—that day they buried my mother I already loved her enough for her death to cut a gash across my heart that never healed, and that led finally to this book, a collection of mysteries and dreams. For most of my life I was searching for something that I could never name. When I began to hear Peggy's voice and to write this book, I realized that I had been searching for her. But the moment the book arrived from the publisher and I saw my father's photograph on the cover, I knew that I had also been searching all my life for a way to thank him. To thank him for not giving up his life. To thank him for going on in the world. For living for me and my brother.

Don J. Snyder
Spring, 2000
Scarborough, Maine

But so with all, from babes that play
At hide-and-seek to God afar,
So all who hide too well away
Must speak and tell us where they are.
—ROBERT FROST, "Revelation"

BOOK ONE

Chapter One

Someday, if we live long enough, we will tell our love stories to a stranger from down the hall, inventing what we must to explain the rush of time and the uncertainty of our place in this world. By then we will have forgotten what we once simply chose not to remember—the slamming door, an angry glance from across the room, the cutting blade of a sentence—and in the telling of our stories we will see again, or for the first time, how blessed our hearts were to have loved at all.

But who will tell our love story when it outlives us?

Or when it drifts beyond the reach of memory?

Who will see you under starlight laying your head upon his shoulder? Who will watch you leading a child through the snow or dipping a new baby's feet into the sea?

And what if we outlive our love story?

Who will hold our old dreams up into the light at dawn again or remind you of the afternoon when you took a daughter into the city to buy her first ballet shoes?

And who will rescue us from the deep, perplexing loneliness of life?

If I see her leaning on her cane, I will remind her how she used to take the front stairs two at a time to reach their bedroom, to take her place beside him.

Find the blond-haired boy whose father taught him to throw a football.

Summon the friend she drove through the night to sit with and persuade of his worthiness.

And if the tree that held the tire swing is gone, even if they've erected a bank teller machine where it stood, stay there a moment anyway, and remember her showing you how to pump your legs and fly above her head.

Let someone dream us all back to life someday. Back to the blue kitchen where you rolled out your pie crust. Back to the fireplace you lit at dusk against the autumn chill. Back to the roof you hammered down in a thunderstorm when lightning raced along the heads of the nails.

I have been dreaming my mother back this way, going back across the years that lay between us to run my hands over her love story. It is a story that was buried with her in the August heat of Pennsylvania in 1950, sixteen days after she gave birth to me and my twin brother. She was nineteen years old, and until last year I never knew anything about her, where she was buried, who her friends were, how she had died, what it was she stood for.

I began searching for her because my father, her husband of less than ten months, is an old man facing his own end. Let me say that for fifty years of his life the pain of missing her prevented him from remembering. And now that he would like to recall her, would like to tell me about her, the tumor in his brain precludes this.

It seems preposterous to me now that I would live almost fifty years after my mother died and still know nothing about her. But this story I am telling here, her love story with my father, could never be told by anyone but me because it was never remembered. Because it was too exquisite in its beginning, too terrible in its end, and the time between the beginning and the end was too brief, it had to be forgotten then. Or, let me say it more precisely, it had to be unremembered. That is it then—an unremembered love story, true in every aspect, preserved behind the heavy door that was closed against the sadness of its end.

I am telling her story now for my father, an old man who was the boy who loved her. And for her, the girl who was my mother. And for you if you are in love, or out of it, or trying to stay in love with the person you have pledged yourself to.

Let us hope that we are all preceded in this world by a love story, that it lies behind us like a shadow, waiting only for us to turn and face it. And in facing it, face ourselves, perhaps.

It was a slow turn on my part. And it began on a winter night in Maine. I was up late with a sick child who, in her fever, kept asking me for a doll that I had not seen in years. Our children's desires so often oppose our own; because she had awakened me from a deep sleep and because I had to be up early the next morning, I wanted to make this middle-of-the-night dance a quick fox-trot, but in my daughter's clear, wide eyes I could see that what she wanted was a slow waltz.

For a while I tried to placate her—a glass of juice, a Popsicle she could take back to bed with her. Nothing worked. Finally, I wrapped her in a comforter and carried her up the attic stairs. As we searched beneath the eaves I felt the heat of her fever through the blanket, and when the only dolls we found were no better than distant relatives of the one she missed so hopelessly, she began to cry. A soft cry of plain disappointment.

"Please don't wake your brother and sisters," I whispered to her.

On the attic floor next to the Christmas-tree stand, which still had a few green needles in its cup, there was a pair of black leather boots worn by her oldest sister, then the middle one, and now waiting for this daughter to step into them. Boxes everywhere. When we opened the one closest to us a photograph fell to the floor. I shined the flashlight on it, an old black-and-white picture of a wedding couple sitting in the back seat of their honeymoon car. My father had sent it to me at Christmas in a box of presents for the children. This year the gifts astonished us, so mismatched were they to the growing children in our midst: a golf club a foot too short for Jack, a dress that would have fit Erin two years earlier when my father last beheld her. My father's purchases spoke of the great distance and the long spaces between visits that separated me from him.

There was that troubling distance and the thievery of time. On the back of the wedding picture my father had written in the child's cursive that had marked his letters since a brain tumor began to steal his faculties—November 1949, Peggy and me.

I watched my daughter take the photograph in her hand. It stopped her crying as she held it to the light.

Then she pressed it against my cheek. "It's Granddad," I said. "That's your grandfather when he was a boy."

A gust of wind raced along the roof above our heads.

There is always one child who drives a harder bargain than the others, whose mouth is forever filled with questions and who charges through the world past flustered grownups.

She wanted to know who the pretty girl in the wedding car was.

"My mommy," I said.

She looked back at the picture as I described for her how this girl used to visit me when I was a little boy. I would awaken from my sleep to the sound of someone calling my name. It was always only the faint whisper of a voice calling me, and always calling me by my first and middle names, the way no one else ever addressed me, and when I opened my eyes there was always the same bright, smiling face with the shining gold ringlets of hair, gliding across my bedroom on top of a column of white light.

It was just an old picture in the attic, a lowly assertion of my daughter's history, and we might have gone downstairs then, leaving it behind, but Cara kept it in her hand. I forgot about it until later that week when it turned up on the table in the kitchen where we keep the unpaid bills, the schools' lunch menus, and the telephone directory. I was looking down at the photograph when my brother called me from his home in southern New Hampshire. He had just returned from Pennsylvania where he spent a day with my father and found him to be confused and going blind. "I wouldn't expect him to live more than another year," he said.

My brother is not given to exaggeration and so I took what he said to heart. I'd hung up the telephone, when I caught myself turning over the photograph to my father's written words on the back:

November 1949, Peggy and me.

I felt the vulnerability we feel when our parents fall to deathly illness, taking our immunity from harm along with them. I sat at the table a long time. When my son, Jack, came into the room I drew him into my arms and waited for the feeling to pass.

That was a year ago, before I knew anything about my mother, Peggy Lorraine Schwartz. Before I knew that she spent the war years learning to drive a car and walk a straight line in high heels. She wore her hair like Ginger Rogers and spent whole weekends with her Sunday school class sewing bandages for the Red Cross. She rode the Liberty Bell trolley to Lansdale to stand outside the recruitment center with her girlfriends and wish good luck to all the boys before they went inside. Sometimes the boys would take off their hats, lean down, and innocently kiss the girls on their foreheads. She went to Saturday-night dances to raise money for Civil Defense. A dime a dance. She was the prettiest girl in town and never sat out a single number. Men twirled her across the floor and she became aware of her beauty for the first time. One hot summer night in 1944, she went with her friends to sleep out in the country in the backyard of a girl named Lorraine Pugles. They laid their sleeping bags under the stars. At four in the morning Lorraine's father woke them up to ride with him to pick up fruit and vegetables, which he sold at a stand in Souderton. The girls all sat in the back of his truck, their bare legs hanging out, their feet on the bumper. Mr. Pugles beeped the horn each time before he came to a bump in the road. They were singing that silly song about the bugle boy in company B. Laughing. Laughing so hard. Peggy with her deep, rolling laugh that the rest of them still remember about her. They told me that Peggy was a quiet girl, always drifting off on her own, lost within her thoughts, but she could laugh when she felt like it. It was a big, strong, unlady-like laugh and they remembered her laughing that night in the back of Mr. Pugles's truck as she stood up and danced the jitterbug with an imaginary soldier. She danced right over the bumps in the road, until they were all rolling on the floor of the truck, laughing along with her. That night of the sleep-over, before they took the ride, when the night was still around them, Lorraine told Peggy about a boy who had gone off to war. He was the only boy she ever went out with who wrote her letters the day after each date, thanking her and telling her how special everything was to him. Lorraine spoke his name, Dick Snyder. Peggy was fourteen years old that summer. Until that night she would remember the war years as a song, as people gathered around radios, and women wearing pants to work. And her father in the backyard search-ing the night sky for enemy planes. Now she added to these memories the name of a soldier who wrote letters to his girl after each date.

This is the boy she would one day decide that no one else should have but her. The boy she would marry and then leave behind. He would never really know who she was or how she loved him. Until I found her for him. Peggy Lorraine, the girl he missed so desperately after she died. He spent the days after her funeral lying in bed, trying to make a bargain with God. Thinking of the countless people who had come near her in the nineteen years of her life. People he would never know. Someone who spoke four words to her in the line at the grocery store. And someone who stood on the corner next to her waiting for the light to change. All of these people, strangers to him—he wanted the time they had spent with her. He wanted to gather all of these people together and have for himself the sum of all their moments in her pres-ence. If he added up all these moments they might amount to an afternoon that he could have to share with her. To hold her close. He promised God that if He granted him this little bit of time with her, he would never ask for anything else again.

There is another photograph. A picture my grandfather took of my father in front of the Christmas tree in December 1950, four months after Peggy's death. Someone has just told him to smile. Smile, Dick, we have to try to be happy for the babies. Smile. That would have been my grandmother, my Nana, telling him to smile. I am guessing at this part. But Pop Pop would have been holding the camera, concentrating too hard on holding it still and centering the picture in the viewfinder to say anything to my father. My twin brother and I are in my father's arms. He has a stunned look on his face, as if he has just been hit by something from behind. Or felt a trapdoor snap open beneath his feet. I am on his right knee. Dave, on his left. We are by now four months old, just old enough to sit up. We are the babies Peggy Lorraine gave him in the tenth month of their marriage and then left him to care for on his own.

I was seven or eight years old when I began to sense some connection between my father and the woman who visited my bedroom at night on the column of white light. We had gone on a family vacation to Cooperstown, New York, that summer to visit the Baseball Hall of Fame. We stayed in a little roadside place called the Wagon Wheel Motel. The first night we were there, my brother and I were enchanted to discover that from the front porch we could see the screen of a drive-in miles away across a valley and up a broad hillside.

It wasn't the first night, maybe the second or third, when I was watching with my father as a luscious black-haired woman in the movie stepped into the tender embrace of a man, then wrapped her slender arms around him in an act of such physical hunger that my father rushed me off the porch. (The actress might have been Natalie Wood.) I can still feel his hand on the back of my head, gently steering me inside the room and into bed. I lay there a long time pretending to be asleep but watching to see if he went back outside. My stepmother was making us a bedtime snack, I remember. My father was walking back and forth, passing the foot of my bed. When at last he announced that he was going outside to smoke, I felt my heart begin to race. After he had passed through the open doorway and I could see his back was to the room, I sat up in bed and watched. For what, I didn't know. There was his slender, hipless outline, his shadow from the porch light falling behind him across the carpeted floor. Out across the grass and the tiny swimming pool and the cracked cement shuffleboard lanes, across the highway, beyond a stand of trees, and the wide sea of the hillside, the woman on the drive-in screen, a giant looming over my skinny father, was saying something to the actor in her arms while my father and I secretly tried to read her lips. I sensed at that moment that we were in this together. The woman on the drive-in screen was the one we both longed for, the one without whose touch our own worthiness would forever be in doubt. In that moment I felt supremely satisfied in some depthless part of me. I felt close to my father in the way I would only feel as a boy whenever he stood off from the rest of us, dreaming—as I imagined he was—about my mother, who was lost to him; dreaming—as I imagined he always did—of some ransom he could pay to God so he could have his pretty bride back. In those days we were conspirators. He dreamed of her, and I waited in my sleep for her to return and call to me by my first and middle names.

Chapter Two

A week passes, maybe two. I have brought the wedding photograph into a sunstruck kitchen to draw my family to it; I want to show Jack how much chrome was on the old cars, and Cara how there is a little bit of her face in my father's. I want to show Erin how Peggy styled her hair. But weekends are busy times in a family of six and my intentions are lost to the normal transactions of a happy Saturday morning. Jack, age nine, sails a paper airplane across the room; it hits me on the bridge of my nose with a surprising pain as I am crossing the floor and makes me spill a cup of coffee down my leg. I am just about to shout at him, but when I pick up the airplane I notice he has written across one wing, "I love you, Daddy. Can we play football today. Check yes or no."

Erin, our twelve-year-old, is on the telephone trying to make plans for an outing with her friend from sixth grade; she is talking with her friend and negotiating with me for some money for lunch at the same time I am cleaning up the spilled coffee. Why seven dollars for lunch? I ask. I've eaten peanut butter and jelly sandwiches for lunch every day for thirty years, why can't I make you one?

Meanwhile Nell, age ten, charges through the room chased by Cara, who is pulling her stuffed animals behind her on a makeshift sled that tips over the dog's water bowl. If this were one of those old movies starring Fred MacMurray, the washing machine would suddenly overflow.

I slip the photograph into my shirt pocket and surrender to it all, leaning back against the kitchen counter while the voices wash over me. I see all the commotion around me, but the picture of my mother and father is drawing me away from all of this. I have fallen onto a peculiar ground of stillness, like the stillness just before a snowstorm.

Colleen appears next, her cheeks rosy from sleep. I am watching her from far away as she calmly gathers up dirty laundry, softly interrogating each of her children to find out if they've seen her sunglasses. When she passes by me her hair is red in the slanting light. In the next moment I watch her kneel down to tie the laces on Cara's shoe. "I don't like my face anymore," Cara announces.

"It's a beautiful, beautiful face," Colleen assures her.

The room grows quiet. The other children have turned to watch their mother.

You know this feeling we get when our life is suddenly orbiting us like a rich dream, this desire to freeze everything just as it is—to rescue one perfect moment from the rushing blur of time. It's a feeling that comes from a sudden recognition of our privilege. How lucky, how fortunate I am, and please let it slow down, let this privilege last!

The urgency behind this feeling comes today from the photograph; there was another woman so young and beautiful, and a man who loved her, never thinking that she would die.

In the stillness, I am vowing to myself to begin living more thoughtfully. I will try harder to remember when I first saw the red in Colleen's hair. I will picture her as she first appeared to me when I fell in love with her. I will remember which of our babies was born with their eyes opened wide. And which daughter named our dog. And which summer we taught our son to swim. I will slow my life down so that I can remember these things. And though we cannot begin to account for the way so much time has passed, or to say precisely how we have become the family we are, I will pull everyone closer to me and hold them there long enough to guard our closeness against the magnificent, hectic future ahead when the velocity of our lives will carry us off in different directions, each of us flying away at top speed, barely glancing back, scarcely remembering.

Here we are, so many of us, standing in our middle age at the end of a century, trying our best to give our children a love story to follow. *Our* love story, more urgent than our daily battle for time and money.

I am watching Colleen and thinking that I will never leave her side again, that I will spend every hour of every day beside her so that I will have this in case she ever gets sick and dies. I remember how frightened I was with each new baby, scared that something would go wrong in the hospital and I would lose her. These are strange thoughts for such a beautiful Saturday morning. I smile at my wife when she comes across the room toward me. She takes the photograph from my hands and holds it in front of her. "What do you remember?" she asks me.

For days I've been thinking about this, trying to remember everything. Every Christmas my father would take us to Hatfield, to visit Grandmom and Granddad Schwartz. They were just kind old people to me. We'd sit in their tiny living room and open our presents, and I was never really sure who they were. Somehow I thought that my father was my older brother and that these old people were his parents. Their daughter, Audrey, lived in the house and there were pictures of her everywhere. But on the top shelf beside the fireplace there were photographs of two girls in silver frames. I remember this distinctly. The silver frames stood beside a white porcelain horse with a gold chain for its bridle.

"You remember that?" Colleen asked.

"Photographs," I told her. "As a kid I always paid a lot of attention to pictures because I was always trying to find the face of the lady who visited me in my room at night."

Soon after we met I had told Colleen about the time my father drove my brother and me to Atlantic City for a day on the beach. I was small, maybe five years old. There was a strong undertow, I remember. We drank orange soda in thick glass bottles. It was the first time in my life I got water up my nose and in my ears. My father showed me how to tilt my head and jump up and down on one leg. When it was time to leave, we walked along the boardwalk and stopped at the outdoor shower, which was a garden hose hanging from a nail inside a wooden stall. It cost a nickel to wash off the sand. After I was finished, as my father took off his shirt to step under the hose, his wallet fell from his pocket and a photograph dropped to the ground. It was a black-and-white picture of the lady who visited me. There she was, sitting at the open window of a big black car with wide, sweeping fenders and hubcaps that were bright disks of light.

I looked into my father's eyes and asked him who she was. I think that even as I was asking him this, I was disappointed in myself for divulging my secret and fearful that now that it was out in the open she wouldn't come to see me again. But it was the exact face that glided in through the window on top of the column of white light. I told my father that I had seen the lady before. He looked down at me with a puzzled expression but didn't say anything else. He just washed the sand off my feet with the hose. He waited a few more years until I was eight or nine, and then he told me that she had been my mother.

"I've been thinking about something," I said to Colleen. "What if I went to Pennsylvania and tried to find out everything I could about Peggy. I mean if I could tell my father his own love story now that he can't remember it. It could be a gift I give to him, while there's still time. I think I owe him that."

Colleen gave me back the photograph. "You owe it to yourself, too," she said.

I didn't see it like that. Not then anyway.

Chapter Three

That winter I was on the road, traveling a hundred miles from home each week to teach at a small college. I would leave the house early Monday morning, spend two nights in a motel, then drive home Wednesday night. A true roadside motel, one where you can sit outside the door to your room in a little plastic chair, put your feet up on the bumper of your car, and watch the traffic pass. In such a place your life can feel temporary and no more complicated than the three or four things you line up on the glass shelf above the bathroom sink. Or what you put on the bedside table.

I always placed the photograph there, standing it up against the ceramic lamp. It had become something more real in my life than what was bringing me to the motel each week. When I was home one weekend Cara put it beside her on her bedside table. I had already left on Monday morning and was in town putting gas into the car when I remembered and drove all the way back home and took it from Cara's table.

I felt self-conscious about it and glad that I had managed to retrieve the photograph and leave the house again without being seen. And that night in the motel I was thinking how I would explain this to anyone, what logic or reason I could have summoned to make it seem like it wasn't the beginning of an obsession. I was lying on the bed watching fat snowflakes land on the roof of my car, when the telephone rang on the bedside table. It was Jack calling to tell me that he had scored a goal in his hockey game that evening. I made him describe the play in slow motion so I could see him in my mind breaking in from the blue line with the puck on his stick, driving hard to his right, white shavings of ice spraying from his blades, then wheeling across the face of the goal, holding the puck out toward the goalie, tantalizing him with it until, at the precise second when the goalie drops down to reach for it, he snaps his stick and sails the puck into the upper right corner of the net.

"I wish you'd been here," he told me.

"I won't miss any more games," I said. It was what I needed to say for my own sake more than his. I'm a busy man with four children whose lives I need to be a part of. I don't need to be searching the past, I need to be living right now in the present tense where my children live so that they don't have to go searching their past someday to find out who the hell *I* was.

I could balance the scales this way until I glanced at the photograph again, or until I shut off the light and tried to fall asleep with my brother's warning banging inside my head.

Even then, it isn't easy to acknowledge certain things. We tell ourselves what is obviously true—*that we don't have forever*—but until we feel this in some deep part of ourselves, we go on with our busy lives, leaving the truth behind while we worry about the balance in our checking account.

I felt it the next night when I was driving home on a back road in the northern part of Maine. I felt a longing to decide something and to set it down in front of Colleen, to put words to the feeling in order to make it real before it could vanish again. I was dreaming myself home, already by her side, when I saw bright lights way out ahead, off in the distance, like a halo washed across the dark sky. I was feeling the loneliness of the road and this cheered me, the thought that the lights might be the town where I had attended college. I drove faster, eager to come upon that friendly town again. But soon the lights up ahead became too bright to be that small town and my spirits began to sink. And then I came upon it—a Wal-Mart standing high up on a hill, surrounded by the blinding arc lights that one associates with prisons. I pulled off to the side of the road and stared at the cinder-block monstrosity and I could not account for why it made me feel so empty. It was crazy, I know, but I started to wonder if all of us have been diminished in some vital way by the age in which we are living, an age when Wal-Marts are summoning us from hillsides across the republic. Did our mothers and fathers hold something fine between them that has been lost to us? Those young people in the old black-and-white photographs, were they trying to warn us of something? Were they trying to tell us that if we weren't careful we might reach a point where much of the fabric of what had always been perceived to be good in America we'd left behind somewhere, left it behind thoughtlessly, without making a choice, and we had become a people cast out, or *lured* out of our own lives into this new landscape where the only thing familiar to us is the artless chain of roadside stores, motels, and restaurants.

I thought again of Colleen at home and about the landscape of our life. Could I possibly lose her? Was there a time coming when I might lose her and never find her again in the dark countryside, the way my father had lost my mother? There they were in their wedding-car photograph, so fit and fine and so blind to the end that was rushing to meet them.

Those moments on the side of the road before the blazing Wal-Mart made me feel like taking hold of something meaningful.

I began to drive hard through the black night, all the elaborate purposes of my life, all the false starts and wrong turns distilled to the one simple act of reaching home. I kept pressing down hard on the accelerator but for some reason I was unable to close the distance; the miles seemed to be dividing and multiplying while I was frozen in place on a road that kept moving out ahead of me, pouring out of itself and spreading farther and farther into the distance.

In the long succession of dark, empty miles I began to feel my father's loss. The loss of hope and love and youth and promise. The loss of immunity. Coming upon my driveway, I pulled the car to a stop and hurried up the porch stairs.

Home.

The dog greets me at the door and leads me through the dark rooms to the kitchen where Colleen has left the stove light on and a plate of food in the refrigerator. I eat standing at the sink, already losing some of the resolve I had felt on the dark highway. This is where we are. Isn't it enough just to be here and to feel the privilege of our life? Who, throughout history, could have had it any better than we do now? How sweet this life of ours, busy and fast and, yes, there is plenty for us to worry about, and we may curse the shallowness of this age and the Wal-Marts riding like cruise ships along the horizon, but hell, it is all so fine, isn't it? I feel myself standing shoulder-to-shoulder with every other husband and wife who are opening their eyes to the end of a century and gazing across their best intentions and their most exquisite failures to the silent borders of time. All we need is to love each other in the best way. To see our children joyful in our closeness. Surely nothing matters more to us than this.

Then I walk out into the living room and pause at the bottom of the stairs. When the house is this quiet I can hear my children breathing in their sleep. How fit and essential is this sound that seems to carry the rhythm of a slow and meaningful journey, a rhythm that sets the house trembling to its cadence.

The dog and I go reverently from bed to bed, kissing a blessing to each sleeping child until, at last, I am standing in the presence of my wife's plain beauty, her face on the pillow, the magazine she was reading on the floor, a night-light left on. The dog finds her place beneath my desk. I take off my shirt and drape it over a chair. There is moonlight on the floor and when I step through it I am suddenly surrounded again by that startling stillness. It seems as if every object in the room has just settled behind a gust of wind that has cleared away everything between me and an understanding of what I must do next in this world: the beautiful woman on the drive-in movie screen far away across the valley and up the hillside, the woman whose voice I tried to hear forty years ago, I have followed to this woman who is humming dreamily to herself as I lean against her. I can hear my wife hold her breath when I lay my palms against her soft skin. For a long time neither of us moves. I feel we are caught then in both the slow shadow of history and the sudden turn of fate.

Chapter Four

After that night I gave myself over to it.

For years I had kept journals for each of my children, which began with a description of their birth and continued on until they were six or seven, when all the pages were filled. Only Cara's had blank pages left, and on the first of these pages I wrote that I was going to go searching for her grandmother. I taped the wedding-car photograph on the same page. I stood up to put the journal on her shelf and when I glanced down again at the photograph it was like I was seeing it for the first time. It is a square, four-inch-by-four-inch picture dominated by the two-inch-by-two-inch car in the center foreground. The car is parked along the right side of the street, facing away from the viewer, a front and rear tire up against the curb. To the left, across the narrow street, stand two large wood-frame houses with porches and overhanging porch roofs in front and wide wooden front steps that descend to the sidewalk.

In the background of the photograph, toward the end of the sidewalk that leads away from the viewer, perhaps fifty feet of actual distance ahead of the wedding car, there is a boy. I had not seen him before because he is wearing a dark double-breasted coat that is rendered shapeless against the dark background of the picture. The collar is turned up and

conceals all but his chin. He has his hands in his coat pockets.
The cuffs of his trousers fall over his shoes. His light-colored
hair is pushed to the right across his forehead. A man, perhaps
his father, is walking just ahead of him, but the boy has
stopped and completely turned around and is looking back at
the wedding car. There is just enough light on the boy's face
to make out his features. He looks to be eight or nine years
old and bears an unmistakable resemblance to me at that age.
In all the photographs of myself that I have ever seen I look
just like him. I closed my eyes and then opened them. Then
again. Each time the boy seemed to be re-entering the photograph, just having stepped into the picture from the blackness
behind him.

The next night I went to each of my children in their beds,
knelt down with the photograph, and asked them who the
boy was. They all said it was me, and only Erin, my oldest
child, questioned the mathematics.

"You weren't born before the wedding," she said. "I don't
get it."

"You're right, it couldn't be me," I told her.

"But it is," she said.

"I know."

I called my father that same night. We talked for a while
about the college football teams that had been chosen for
bowl games. He was a Penn State partisan and he told me that
he wasn't going to miss the game on New Year's Day.

"Maybe I'll watch it with you," I told him.

This didn't register with him. Instead he told me he
had been going to a lot of funerals lately for all his old bud-
dies from his 1944 high school football team. "Just last week

I bumped into Ozzie Newcomb at Ed Slater's funeral. I don't know how much longer Ozzie will live. I don't know how all these big strong boys from the football team can die this way."

He said he still wished that he had been big enough to play football as a boy. Instead he was the team waterboy.

I asked him if it would be all right if I came to see him. "We can watch the Penn State game together," I said again.

"It's a long trip for you."

"Not that long. Eight or nine hours."

"Longer than that, I think."

"It's okay, Dad. I was hoping we could talk a little about Peggy. I thought we might just talk for a little while about her."

"Your mother was working at the telephone company when I met her. She was an operator."

A telephone operator?

My mind went blank for a moment; my father was still talking at the other end but I had drifted far away. When I came back to his voice, it was with the realization that I was forty-seven years old and this was the first concrete detail about her that my father had ever passed on to me. I had never been to her grave, I had no idea how many days she lived after I was born, how old she was when she died, or what had been the cause of her death. Growing up with my father, I had always known in some part of my comprehension that talking about my dead mother was too painful for him. Because she had died when their love was new and they were still in the heat of their passion for each other, her death had cut an opening in him so that he was never the same and he could never speak about her. It is true that we all have a beginning, a middle, and an end to our lives, but they don't always come in that order; even as a young boy I had known through intuition that by the time I knew my father he had already been through the beginning and the end of his life, and he was just living out the long middle part trying not to remember what had already happened to him.

But now he had told me that she worked as a telephone operator. I could picture the girl in the wedding photograph going to work every day, probably sitting in a room full of young women wearing headsets. This simple detail from my father, and the vivid picture it inspired of her *alive* in a life that preceded me, rather than dead at a point in time after I was born, made all the difference.

On New Year's Day I threw a few things into the car and began the drive to Collegeville, Pennsylvania, where my father and stepmother lived. They had moved there after he retired from the ministry nine years earlier but I had never been to see them there and I had to call my brother for directions.

I drove with the photograph on the seat beside me. Since discovering the boy in the picture, I kept expecting to find something new each time I looked at it. The car is polished to a high shine, a reflection of the church steeple is blown across its wide roof. Crepe paper streamers run from the front bumper and over the roof to the fender, which is a gash of bright silver that has caught the flash of the camera. Below the oval rear window that holds their faces is taped a square piece of construction paper with the word JUST at the top and the word MARRIED below. The words are printed by hand, neatly but with no artistic flare. Above the chrome trunk handle is the license plate: 5AJ87. And in smaller letters above the number, 1949 PENNA. A plaque of some sort with the logo of Lehigh University is attached by two screws to the top of the license plate. I wondered whose car this was, who had gone to Lehigh and who was driving the wedding couple.

There is a puddle of water along the sidewalk and some litter in the gutter. On a telephone pole beyond the car the numbers 8 over 30 are stenciled with white paint. The bare branches of a tree are reflected in the polished chrome bumper, as well as a one-story house. It is a gangster car, a big tub of a car with swollen, sweeping fenders and dashes of chrome around all the windows. You cannot imagine going fast in this car, but you can imagine being safe in it.

My father's face reflects this; he looks so sure of himself, so secure in the confidence that nothing bad could ever happen to them. His wide smile of even white teeth, his eyes dancing in light behind the glass of his round wire-rimmed spectacles. All in all he shows the exuberance of a twenty-three-year-old man who has survived the nightmare of a long war and has returned home unharmed to claim the prettiest girl in town for his bride.

Peggy is a different story. She is not looking at the camera as he is. Her eyes have strayed to the left a little. Her mouth is cut off by the lower frame of the rear window, but if she is smiling, there is no trace of it in her eyes, which show a puzzled look, as if she has seen something troublesome. It is an expression that doesn't match the garland of bright flowers in her hair.

I want to know what she sees on that November morning. She has just been married, and she will dance the night away and there is nothing *not* to smile about unless she sees something beyond this moment in time and is looking ahead rather than behind as is her new husband, to another war that will begin before ten months have passed and will take so many boys away again. Maybe even her new husband.

Could she be thinking about the future, about the crazy times just ahead when the newspapers will be filled with stories about communist infiltrators, and a young husband and wife will be arrested in New York City as spies and taken from their two small children to be executed in the electric chair?

Or maybe she has lost a friend in the last war and is thinking of this friend as the shutter of the camera falls, wishing he could be here to see her in her wedding car.

Something *has* distracted her.

I want to see some eagerness in her eyes, an eagerness to finish up with these wedding photographs so that she can be alone with my father. Eager to touch him and for him to touch her.

It is the far-off look in her eyes that makes me wish I could do something to help her.

I drove all the way to Pennsylvania that New Year's Day, wishing I could do something for the people in the photograph beside me. The two of them, already fugitives from a fate that was bearing down on them as this photograph was being taken. A fate that would kill her and rip the trajectory out of his youth so that his life became tied to only one question— *How will I ever go on living?*

There they were at the very beginning of their love story, yet already hurrying toward its end, and I could do nothing for them. I could not prevent them from taking another step closer to their end.

Chapter Five

Our fathers, who art in old age, how we shall come upon them, in pale blue flannel pajama bottoms pulled up too high, far above their waists, the way our own children hiked them up when they were first learning to dress themselves.

"Oh, it's been a sad game," he says to me.

"There was a lot of traffic on the New Jersey turnpike, but I had it on the radio. I'm sorry they lost."

"You must be hungry?"

"No, no, I'm fine, Dad."

"I'll make some coffee."

When he stands up I put my arms around him and he says to the emptiness in this room, "Donnie's here. My boy is here."

"I'm here."

"I'm glad you're here."

A house-worth of furniture lines the walls of these four tiny nailed-together rooms. An avocado-green couch I remember. An embroidered chair I've never seen. The old dining-room table I'd forgotten. "I need to get Ma some new chairs," he tells me. "These are falling apart."

Grateful for something to do, I am soon down on my knees checking the joints of the chairs. "A little glue, but these are great, Dad. You couldn't buy any as nice as these today."

He wanders out of the kitchen. I watch him disappear around the corner saying, "Christmas cookies, Christmas cookies."

Beneath the table I am his little boy again, setting up my Union and Confederate soldiers, moving cannons into place, tying horses to the oak legs. For my fort, a blanket draped across the table, hanging down over the sides. I would wait there for him to come home from the night shift. The best part was remaining perfectly still and silent, watching his shoes cross the floor, coming toward me, then turning away. He would pretend he didn't see me there, making me wait. Then, as if it was the most sensible thing in the world as well as the thing he wanted most to do, he would crawl in beside me with his cup of coffee, the scent of tobacco and Old Spice aftershave filling the fort. "Am I your buddy today?" I would ask him.

Now I hear him banging something in the next room. In the light, when I come upon him, I can see how the tumor has begun to drag down the right side of his face. One eye is nearly closed.

"What's the trouble here, Dad?"

Again he is my own little boy, Jack, at home, trying to stuff his clothes into a bureau drawer that is already full. He tells me that the whole football team is dying—here, this shirt, these sweaters belonged to a halfback and to the tall Polish boy who kicked extra points. "Their wives keep blessing me with their clothes," he tells me. "Look at these beautiful clothes they've blessed me with."

I see a different bureau before me. The one in the basement where he kept his things from the army when I was his little boy. The collapsible wood-handled spade for digging a foxhole. The long green coat so heavy I cannot drag it away, the canvas poncho, the canteen, and the leatherbound Bible every GI was issued. You could fit the Bible in the pocket over your heart, and my father knew stories of these Bibles deflecting bullets. For five or six years I played war with his things until they were lost all over the neighborhood.

We put everything on the bed and fold it carefully. "You need someone who will bless you with a bigger bureau," I tell him.

Like a teenager he sleeps late in the morning. I've been drinking coffee for hours when at last I hear him say, "It's our big day, Donnie."

"Yes, our big day, Dad. Are you sure?"

"Sure?"

"It could be a long day."

"Oh, I'm ready," he says. "This is our day."

After nearly fifty years he is going to take me to the old places. We made a list last night before we went to bed. The dance hall where he and Peggy went on dates, the church where they were married, the apartment where they lived after the honeymoon, the print shop where he worked, the parking lot where her uncle taught her to drive, the telephone company where she worked, the hospital where I was born, the cemetery. These points of their compass are all within an eight-mile radius.

Two miles out on the main road his head is bowed and his eyes are closed. It's the Dilantin he is taking to prevent seizures; it puts him to sleep at the drop of a hat. Oranges, I've been told, will help keep him awake. I follow the signs to Hatfield, peeling an orange in my lap.

The road winds through farmland, past old barns and walls made of stone. I round a corner and suddenly the sky ahead is a riot of color. Two rainbows, perfect spectrums, are rising from the horizon in front of us and sweeping high across the sky. There is no rain or sun, just a pale gray sky, yet the rainbows are brilliant. When I call to my father and wake him to look, his eyes open wide as if he has awakened in heaven.

We pull off the road into a gas station where the mechanics have come out from the garage bays and are looking up into the sky while they wipe grease from their hands.

"I don't see rain anywhere," one of them says.

Everyone is trying to figure out what has happened in the sky above our heads when my father says to me, "I don't remember where I was when I first saw Peggy."

It was my last question to him the night before. He remembers seeing a picture of her at Lauchman's print shop. Her father, who ran a Linotype press beside his, took the picture from his wallet and showed it to him during a morning coffee break.

"You don't have to remember right now," I tell him.

He's angry with himself. "I want to remember," he says. "I want to tell you everything."

"Are you sure?"

"Oh yes. Turn left right here."

Twenty minutes later we are lost, heading in the wrong direction. The rainbows are off to our left now, melting into the pale winter sky.

My father bows his head and mutters, "Dumb. Dumb."

I feel sorry for him and try to cheer him up. "Do you remember the things you used to say to me when I was a little boy? Has your get-up-and-go got-up-and-went?"

He smiles to himself. "Remember this one? 'If you don't behave yourself I'm going to send you to the Colorado School of Mines.'"

He laughs at this. I am driving along and peeling another orange for him and thinking, I'm spending precious time with my father . . . I made him laugh.

Coming into Hatfield now, he sits up straight and looks around thoughtfully, as if someone has called his name suddenly.

He points out where the train station used to stand. And the lumber and coal yard where he and Peggy's father got the materials to build his house on School Street. The old Army-Navy recruiting station used to be there on the corner. And the Hatfield Consolidated School where Peggy went through all twelve grades.

"When did she graduate?" I ask.

He does the mathematics in his head. "She worked for the telephone company in 1949. We were married that year. So, she must have graduated in 1948. Yes, 1948."

Just a few blocks from the school we pass a church, then turn left onto Market Street. "There," he says. I stop in front of a duplex house, pale pink. There are five electric meters screwed to the side of the house by the entrance. Apartments.

"It was a house when your mother and I lived there."

"When?"

"Before you were born. It was your grandparents' house; when Peggy got too sick to take care of herself, we left our own apartment in Lansdale and moved in here with Peggy's mother and father. Her grandfather and grandmother lived in one half of the house, along with an aunt. We lived in the other half with her mother and father. And of course your uncle Jack, he was a little boy then, and his sister Audrey who was born just a few months before you boys."

I am watching him closely to see if this is too difficult.

He tells me that Peggy got very heavy and was filling up with fluids. When you touched her, it was like she was filled with wet sand, your finger left an impression.

"The hospital where she died, and the cemetery where she's buried, are they near here?"

Maybe he hasn't heard me. "I'll show you the church," he says.

Hatfield is a town whose streets you could memorize the first time through. A few shops downtown. The old granite bank building at the traffic light. Tiny houses with little front and back yards line all the streets, brick row houses built quickly to accommodate the troops coming back from the war. A huge new generation of babies conceived in their little rooms.

"There must have been pregnant women everywhere you went," I say to myself.

"Your grandmother just had Audrey before we moved in," he tells me.

I guess I already knew this, but now with the picture of the tiny house in mind, it strikes me how impossible it must have been—my father and his pregnant sick wife, her father and mother and their newborn daughter and their little boy. The grandparents and an old aunt. All packed into the place on Market Street in the summer of 1950. And after August 11, add me and my twin brother to the population.

"The noise level alone must have been something," I say.

"Your mother had terrible headaches. I used to put wet washcloths across her forehead, I remember."

We pull up against the curb in front of the brick church while he is telling me how Peggy would sit up in bed with her hands clamped over her ears.

It's the telephone pole up ahead of where we've parked that makes me take out the wedding-car photograph. The pole marked by the same numbers 8 over 30 stenciled in white. By chance we have parked in exactly the same spot where their wedding car was parked for the photograph. I am about to tell this to my father when he says, "This is where the hearse was parked. I remember."

It sweeps over him then, the great faraway look of weariness which my boyhood memorized.

I am trying to banish his memory of the hearse. "Here," I keep insisting, holding the wedding-car photograph in front of him. "The picture you sent me, Dad. Look. See the two houses across the street? There? And the telephone pole? It's exactly the same. Nothing has changed. Look, count the front steps coming down from the porches. See?"

Suddenly he tilts his head back. Light from the sky fills the lenses of his glasses so I can no longer see his eyes. He asks me what time it is. "We don't want to be late for dinner," he says.

I tell him we have plenty of time. But I can see we aren't going to make it to the hospital where Peggy died, or to the cemetery. I see that the past is not about time at all really. The past is a place. Right here where the hearse was parked. *Here* is the past.

"Maybe we *should* head back," I say.

When I start up the car he places his hand on my right arm and thanks me. "I can't remember where we used to go on dates. You asked me last night, and I can't remember. I can't remember where I first met your mother either. I used to know the answers to all those questions, but now I can't remember."

"It's okay," I tell him.

"But I do remember that your mother and I weren't together the last night of her life. She wanted to sleep in her mother's bed. She had your granddad carry her to her mother's bed, I remember. And at the funeral, riding to the cemetery, I kept thinking about that."

I see the tears standing in his eyes. I get the car moving and peel another orange for him, and all I want to do is tell him something that will make his tears go away. I want to tell him that everything is going to be okay, that even with the pain and the awful memories, we'll be all right.

We talk about football that night. It's as close as we can get to anything real. He dreamed of playing football from the time he was five years old. High school and then college football. But he was too skinny. When the Depression came along his family was forced to move, but it was a fortuitous move for him because he ended up in a duplex right next door to Jack Graham, captain of the Lansdale High School football team. Jack took the skinny kid under his wing, introduced him to all the important kids, the pretty girls, the football coach who gave him the job as waterboy. Just to be down on the field during the games was a thrill. Just to be that close to it.

In the morning he makes me breakfast before I leave. Someone from church has sent him grapefruit and oranges from Florida and he insists on cutting up some for me. A bowl of fruit. I'm watching him trying to figure it all out, the right bowl, the knife, a dish towel to wipe the counter. Starting over, beginning with the orange this time. Where to put the seeds. It takes almost an hour.

At the door we shake hands. He says a prayer that God will keep me safe on the drive home. From the parking lot I look back and see him standing at the door of the apartment building. It reminds me of myself standing outside the front door on Clearspring Road waiting for him to come home from work, to beep the horn once the way he always did when he spotted me there. Thinking of it—what the sound of his horn and the sight of him coming home from work meant to me! I want to take him back to Maine with me. I want to sit him in the wing chair in my living room, in front of the fireplace with all the kids gathering around him. Just keep him in my presence.

Chapter Six

A month passes before I can make another trip down the same highways. I have spoken by telephone with an aunt of my mother's who was very close to her. And two girls from her high school class. Pieces of my mother's life are falling into my own.

Before I drive to my father's apartment this time, I return to Hatfield first, back to the same spot at the curb where the wedding car and the funeral hearse had parked. It is a Sunday morning and on the patch of grass in front of Grace Lutheran Church a young man in a stiff blue suit is changing the letters inside the glass cupboard that tells the times of Sunday school classes and the title of the weekly sermon. He is spelling out next week's sermon one black magnetic letter at a time, and watching me out of the corner of his eye. "The Gift of Grace" is the title. He locks the cupboard with a padlock, glances at me again, then disappears inside the church.

A few minutes pass before a young woman comes down the front steps of the church. The man in the blue suit returns. He says something to her and they both turn to look at me. There is suspicion on his face. He checks the padlock again. We live in crazy times; I suppose someone might break into the glass cupboard and change the letters of the sermon title to spell some obscenity. The young woman at his side is lovely. She has come outside with no coat on and there is something interesting about her dress. It is pale pink, ruffled, with puffy short sleeves and a big bow in back. A child's Easter dress and she is spilling out of it.

She walks down the cement walkway and up to the car. She has a movie-star face with rouged and sculpted cheekbones, wide-set blue eyes, lots of curls. I roll down the window. She wants to know if she can help me. She leans into the car window a little, her breasts resting against the bottom of the window frame. I am already trying to think of what I can say so she won't try to get me to join her church. I imagine that her stunning beauty once led her down the road to a wayward life, but now she is reformed and always on patrol for others who appear lost.

I tell her quickly why I am here. That my mother was photographed in her wedding car outside this church in 1949, and a few days after my twin brother and I were born, she was in a hearse parked here. I show her the photograph. She studies the picture, then her eyes open wide.

"Wait a second," she says. "What was your mother's name?"

When I tell her, everything falls into place. "Yes," she says, "the young mother with twin boys. Someone puts flowers on the altar for her every year, the same Sunday every August."

"She died in August," I tell her. She listens to me with a serene and benevolent expression. I am looking into her eyes when the man in the stiff blue suit comes for her. He stops on the cement walkway and calls for her. She smiles and wishes me luck. When she walks away the thought that I will never see her again fills me with an unreasonable sadness.

"The flowers," I call to her. "Who gives the flowers for the altar every year?"

She turns back to tell me she doesn't know.

. . .

It is a twenty-minute drive to the town of Sellersville where
the ambulance took my mother in the last hours of her life.
But coming upon Grandview Hospital, I see that the building
is too modern, too new to be the right place.

The glass doors slide open to a foyer with tall floor-
to-ceiling windows, an immaculate room furnished with
comfortable chairs and couches. The place is deserted, the
information desk unoccupied and the glass-fronted interior
offices empty. The men's room floor has been polished with
something that gives off a familiar sweet smell and I stand
there until I remember that the bathrooms in my elementary
school smelled exactly like this.

Out in the corridor now I can hear someone typing on a
keyboard beyond the silence. She is a pleasant woman with a
quick smile. "I'm holding down the fort," she tells me.

When I ask her where the old Grandview Hospital is, she
walks to a window and points to a square three-story building
across a parking lot. "It is a nursing school now," she tells me.

Walking toward the building I think of the nursing students filling the rooms. Someone up late at night studying for
an exam. Someone far from home looking out the window
my mother once looked out.

Of course, because of the weekend the building is empty
and the front doors are locked. I knock anyway, then step
back to take it in. The doors are set back, up three steps, just
inside an alcove, a rectangle made of rose granite. Cracks
have been filled in with blond cement. The windows on all
three floors are framed in granite as well. Above the center
windows on the second floor the words nurses' home are
carved in tall scrolled letters. There is a flat roof above the
third floor.

Around the back of the building just outside a rear door there is a picnic table. Cigarette butts beneath it.

Peering in through the glass door I see a man walking the corridor pushing a broom. It takes him a while to hear me and when he comes to the door he tells me through the glass that the place is closed until Monday morning.

"My mother died here almost fifty years ago, and I've driven all the way from Maine," I tell him. My voice is hoarse but loud, as if yelling into a dark tunnel.

There is that split second of doubt and fear that surrounds all chance encounters with strangers nowadays. But then he lets me in. When I show him the photograph and tell him the story, he raises one finger in the air and tells me to follow him.

Another old photograph, this one from a desk drawer in a first-floor office. We take it outside and he holds it to match our perspective. I feel a chill run through me. The cedar trees in front of us my mother would have seen as she was carried inside. Her last glimpse of the outside world.

"Wait a minute," the man says cheerfully. "I can do better than this."

Inside he makes a telephone call. Then a second call to a woman who used to work here. I am listening to him explaining to the woman why he is calling. ". . . He says his mother died here in 1950."

"August," I tell him. "My mother had just given birth to twins."

He tells her then pauses suddenly. He turns to me, looks out over the tops of his glasses and says, "Twin boys?"

The twins whose mother died; the woman remembers at once.

But we are in the wrong building. The nurses' home was never a hospital.

. . .

Back in Hatfield, I stop at a 7-Eleven to ask directions to the cemetery. A teenager with a nose ring and a ponytail says, "The Lutheran cemetery?"

I'm surprised by this, that a young person would know the religious affiliation of a particular cemetery. "There's more than one cemetery in town?" I ask.

"Down there," he tells me. "Hang a right on Penn Street."

Coming upon it I can see the grave markers in the distance.

A flat stretch of pasture behind a dump of old railroad ties and a rusted-out factory that once made something before America began manufacturing only debt. I park at the entrance and walk in a ways. Many of the graves belong to soldiers. Young boys who died in places far from here. Their graves are marked by tiny American flags. The Peterson boy could have read my mother's name carved in a desk at school. The Schultz boy might have watched her walking through town before he left for the war in France.

Of all things unexpected, I come upon my father's name first. Written on the face of a stone buried flat in the ground. RICHARD SNYDER. My father for certain, the boy whose mother gave him no middle name. It comes as a shock to me that they share a stone. The plot is so narrow, he will have to be buried on top of her.

His name is on the left of the stone and below it, the year of his birth, 1926, and a space awaiting the year of his death. To the right on the same stone, PEGGY L. SNYDER. 1931–1950.

A line of geese crosses the sky. A low breeze makes the tiny flags tremble.

I picture my father on the day of the funeral. How he must have wanted never to leave this place, to crawl into the earth with her, his heart set upon going along with her. My twin brother and me at home a few blocks away waiting for him to return. The house on Market Street so close he could have heard us crying during the funeral service.

I see my father here with his head bowed, his eyes open to the pile of dirt that will cover her.

I kneel down in the brown grass and the pine cones. I have been returning here all my life. I have returned to a place I've never been before. I have come back to a place I never left. It is a place I've been running from all my life, a memory in the center of my bones, a story sewn into my cells, a knowledge beneath the soles of my feet, a scent on my palms, a warning along my shins.

The earth is soft. As I stare at the dates on the marker, the numbers turn in my mind, 1931–1950—until, finally, it strikes me that she was only nineteen years old. Nineteen. A girl.

I'm embarrassed speaking out loud, but I say these words to her: "I don't know where you are, Peggy."

Chapter Seven

In the nursing home the rooms are behind long carpeted corridors of doors the residents have decorated with photographs of the pets they had to leave behind when they were admitted, and grandchildren who live far away in the noisy, chaotic world that is the exact opposite of this world.

My grandfather has white wavy hair and a steady stream of single women who keep tabs on him. He is ninety years old and has a hard time getting up out of his chair, but other than this, age seems to have taken nothing from him. His son, my uncle Jack, has told him that I would be coming by and from the moment I step inside his door the memories of my mother pour out of him. He has photographs for me that I can keep and framed photographs of her standing on every table and windowsill and on the bureau by his bed. "I dust them all myself," he tells me. Just as my mother had been carefully and purposefully withdrawn from his house where I visited him and my grandmother when I was a boy, the two small rooms he inhabits now have been transformed into a gallery of Peggy's face. I wonder if at this point in his life, nearing his own death, he is familiarizing himself with his daughter's face, a face he believes he will see in heaven.

We sit in her presence now. It strikes me how odd she would find the two of us, her tough-guy father, now sobbing like a child, and her newborn baby now grown bald on the top of his head. I look at her father and then at her face frozen in time, trying to imagine how she would look by now at age sixty-six.

"I delivered your mother when she was born, and I was the last person with her when she passed away," he tells me. "She lifted her hands off the hospital bed and brought them to her head like this and cried out to me, 'My head! My head!'"

He puts his face in his hands and begins to cry softly. I haven't seen him since my grandmother's funeral nine years before, and the memories I have of him are standing in his garage workshop surrounded by tools and a shiny new car that he was very proud of.

"We never talked about Peggy," I tell him

He shakes his head. "It was rough," he says.

Once he begins, he goes on and on. He tells me about the time that Peggy saved his life. He remembers that in the last days of her pregnancy her feet were so swollen that she couldn't even fit into his slippers. And her sewing, he remembers the way she would stay up all night sewing baby clothes. And the first time he saw her after Dave and I were born, she told him that after seeing us she had decided she was going to have six boys.

"She didn't know how sick she was," he says as he begins to cry again. This time he battles through the grief until he can think of something else to tell me that will help him find his voice: "Do you know that Dick was helping me build the house on School Street that summer? Every afternoon after work, we'd drive from the print shop straight to School Street. One afternoon we were hurrying to get the roof on before the rain. A big thunderstorm came in. We were still up on the roof and we watched the lightning jump across the heads of the nails . . . Every afternoon when we were driving over I would say a prayer that Peggy was feeling better and might be there waiting for your father and me. Every afternoon that was what I prayed for." He tells me that every year in August he places the flowers at the church altar in Peggy's memory.

When I try to leave, he keeps me another hour standing at the door. He won't say goodbye until I tell him when I will return.

I didn't return the next day as I had promised my grandfather. And I didn't stay in Pennsylvania long enough to visit my father either. The hell of it was that it was just too damned sad; I don't mean for me, I mean for them—for the father who prayed for his daughter to get well and for the ninety-year-old man who Peggy's father had become, and for the young husband coming home from work each afternoon to find his wife still too weak to get out of bed and for the seventy-one-year-old man her husband had become. I had told myself from that first night in the attic with my little girl that I was going to try to learn Peggy's love story and then tell it for my father, as a gift to him at the end of his life. This had felt like the right thing to do until I saw the sadness in his eyes when we were parked in front of the church. It wasn't the wedding that he remembered as we sat there, it was the funeral. How could I have failed to see that it would be this way for my father, that it would always be this way because she never did get well enough to spend much time with him when he was helping her father build his little house on School Street, the house where my brother and I were taken at Christmas every year though we never knew why. Of course the sadness of Peggy's death had eclipsed their love story, and always would in his memory.

And then seeing my grandfather cry, his shoulders shaking as we sat in his room at the nursing home surrounded by pictures of his lost daughter—it was just too damned sad.

Driving home to Maine, north for eight hours, the feeling of returning that I'd had at Peggy's grave was with me again. Maybe we are always returning, and the first step we take, we took long ago. I could still feel this as I stepped onto the moonlit porch of my house. It was midnight. The bare tree branches were rattling in the wind off the sea. It was well below zero and the porch stairs sounded like they were splitting beneath my feet. Above my head, white stars were scattered across a black sky, near enough to show the sharpness of their edges. The same stars from the last night of my mother's life when she lay in her mother's bed, unable to sleep, perhaps sensing the blood storm just ahead of her. And her husband in a separate room lost to grief.

Lost. Lost for so long. Always lost to me.

And maybe better if she were always lost to me.

Maybe it would have been better that way. Or if not better, then certainly easier. One visit to Peggy's grave, a few companionable days with my father.

I was surprised to find Colleen awake when I came upstairs. She was sitting up in bed with her reading lamp on. "I've just had the most wonderful dream," she said to me. "I dreamed that you found Peggy. You were walking down this beautiful road in the country, not just you, but all four of the kids and I were with you. We were calling her name. I could hear Cara with her high-pitched voice calling for Peggy. And then we saw someone up ahead standing on the side of the road. And it was her. She looked exactly the same, she hadn't gotten old, and she said she was waiting for us to take her home with us. She'd been waiting a long time. She took Erin's hand and we all turned around on the road and came home to Maine."

I sat down on the bed and asked her if my father or my grandfather was in the dream. They weren't, she said.

I told her that I was afraid of hurting them and that I had decided to just let things go.

"Audrey called while you were gone," Colleen said.

My mother's sister, who had been born just ten months before my twin brother and I. Ten months before Peggy died. Audrey had never called me in my life, but I knew exactly why she had called. "It's Granddad, isn't it? She found out that I was at the nursing home."

I was right. But it was more than this. "Granddad told her that he was worried about you."

"Worried about *me?* I'm worried about *him.*"

"You didn't go back to see him," Colleen went on. "He made a list of six people for you to get in touch with. But he told Audrey he was worried it might be too sad for you."

I told her that it wasn't sad for me. "I stood at her grave and I didn't feel sad."

"What did you feel?"

"I don't know. Close to her, I guess. I felt like I was finally where I belonged. Right there, next to her."

"It took you a lot of years to get there," she said. "Ever since I met you and you told me about your mother, I've wondered why you didn't try to find out about her or at least find where she was buried. If anything happened to me, I wouldn't want our children to just forget me because it was too sad to remember. And this isn't just about your mother's love story with your father. It's about your love story with her.

The story that's been missing for so long. I think you have a duty to find her story. Even if it makes *everybody* on earth sad. She never had the chance to tell her story to anyone."

I was talking to a dear friend about this a few days later. *Duty,* that was the right word, he agreed. "I'd say it's your solemn duty."

Chapter Eight

It was cold and there was a hard wind blowing. The people out walking along Main Street in Hatfield had their heads bowed low beneath the winter sky. I was standing at a pay phone, watching everyone who passed me, trying to figure out if they were old enough to have been alive when my mother walked these same streets. As I watched them, I had this mounting desire to whisper my mother's name to each of them as they passed, and then to wait to see who would stop and turn around.

From the pay phone I called the number in the directory for Muriel Schwartz. She was Peggy's aunt who, with her husband, Howard, had lived only a few blocks from the little duplex that Peggy's parents rented on Market Street in Hatfield. I'd been told that she and Peggy spent a lot of time together.

On the telephone she said, "In the days after you were born I came by each morning to give you and your brother your baths."

I asked her if I could come see her.

She lived alone in a modern complex of small apartments. She was shivering when I went inside. The winter weather bothered her and she told me that she seldom went outside.

There was a photograph of Howard in a frame by the window and when I saw it, I told her how I had always liked him. Those times I was taken to my grandparents' house on School Street around Christmas, Howard and Muriel were usually there. Howard had seen combat in the war. He was the kind of tough guy who naturally appeals to little boys because he told stories about soldiers, he had big muscles and tattoos on his arms and he would pass my brother and me bottles of Coca-Cola like a conspirator, saying with a sly grin, "Don't tell anyone where this came from, boys." He had died more than ten years ago.

"Are you okay, living here by yourself?" I asked Muriel.

"Oh, I'm fine," she said brightly. "Lonely, I guess. No one prepares you for how lonely life becomes when you get old. But let's talk about Peggy. Do you know your mother at all, Donald?"

"No," I said.

She smiled at me. "Well, it's time that you know her. I'm going to tell you who she was."

I spent a wonderful morning there in her living room. Muriel spoke in soft, measured sentences about my mother's childhood and her high school years when she was becoming a young woman. During those years Muriel had raised three small boys and Peggy was the primary baby-sitter. She helped Muriel care for these boys, and during the war when Howard was gone for three years, Peggy kept Muriel company.

"I considered your mother a close friend," she told me.

The whole time I listened to Muriel, a picture of my mother began to form in my mind. The first clear picture I'd ever had. I felt so close to her that when it was time for me to leave, and Muriel spoke about the last hours of Peggy's life, I felt the loss of my mother for the first time.

It was a Sunday morning and Muriel had come by as she always did to give Dave and me our baths. It was August 27, sixteen days after we were born, Peggy's seventh day home from the hospital.

"The house was empty," Muriel recalled. "It was a Sunday and everyone had gone to church. Your mother had been getting weaker and weaker since she came home after your birth. I never saw her hold you boys, not once. She just didn't have the strength. That morning I had this really spooky feeling when I opened the front door. I can't describe it. It was eerie and I can still remember it. There wasn't a sound in the house. The bed in the sitting room where your mother and father slept was empty. I looked at it and it was the first time I didn't see Peggy there. And I knew that wherever she was, she would have been carried from that bed, she was too weak to walk on her own.

"I found her upstairs in her mother's bedroom. She was curled up on one corner of the bed. Her skin was gray, I will never forget that. Awful . . . She was coughing very faintly. I went over to her and said, 'Oh, Peggy, you're so sick, aren't you?' She looked into my eyes with such . . . I don't know, just like she was crying out to me to please help her.

"I called Dr. Paul Moyer, the family doctor, not the doctor she'd had with you boys. Dr. Moyer arrived shortly, took one look at Peggy and exclaimed, 'This is not the girl I know.' He called for an ambulance while I stayed with Peggy. Her face . . . She looked like the photographs that we had all been seeing in the news of the people in the Nazi concentration camps.

"I went along to the hospital. Your father's good friend, Bill someone . . . I can't remember his last name. He drove me to the hospital.

"They took her upstairs. I was in the waiting room. Your father and grandparents arrived very soon after this. Granddad went upstairs with your father to be with Peggy. She died very shortly after this. No more than an hour after we were together at the hospital.

"Your father came to the waiting room to tell us. It was the oddest thing. He had this terrible look in his eyes, and a faint smile, like he was trying to be brave . . . He was holding Peggy's watch above his head in his right hand. He was walking stiffly across the floor, taking tiny steps. 'At least I have her watch,' he said. 'They let me keep her watch.'

"I knew then," Muriel told me, "that your father might never be the same again."

Chapter Nine

There were days after this when I had to keep a notebook with me everywhere I went. Driving the car, eating a meal with Colleen and the kids, even standing in front of a classroom teaching college students. Peggy's story was such a presence in my mind and my heart that it poured out of me. I began waking at four in the morning to the sound of her voice, and the sentences that I wrote down weren't coming from inside me, but from somewhere far away. The sentences fell onto each page effortlessly. And whenever I felt Peggy's voice growing faint I telephoned one of her friends from high school whose names my grandfather had given me.

I was exhilarated by each new page. And then I was certain that I should throw the pages away so they would never see the light of day.

Because of my father. Because of the sadness at the center of Peggy's story. For the same reason my father had never spoken to me and my brother about her, I was now convinced that I should let her voice remain silent, locked beyond the heavy door of sorrow that my father and my grandparents and everyone else had closed when Peggy died.

· · ·

My mother's brother, Jack, came to see me in Maine not long after this. I hadn't seen him in fifteen years. He was sixty years old now and to our astonishment we looked so much alike, we could have been brothers. We walked the beach in Scarborough that day. The waves, when they rose up into the light just before they broke, were a lovely enamel green. I told Jack that I had spoken with his father and with Muriel and that I had begun writing pages but wasn't sure I should take it any further.

"Why not?" he said.

I gave him what was becoming my stock reply, that if I kept going, I was bound to bring back all the sadness again. The sadness that my grandfather and my father had spent their lifetimes trying to outrun.

"Have you asked your dad how he feels about it?"

"Not directly," I said. "I just don't want to bring him any sadness now, at this time in his life." I was staring out to sea as I said this to Jack. It was that time of late afternoon when there is a moment of stillness along the shore, just before the last slanting light disappears beyond the high dunes. In that moment I realized something, but I couldn't say anything because Jack was suddenly telling me about the day Peggy died.

"I was riding my bike across the street at Snyder's coal and lumber yard. One of the neighbors came across the street and said, 'Your sister was taken to the hospital this morning.' I said, 'I know that.' You know the way a twelve-year-old kid doesn't want to let on that he doesn't know everything there is to know about everything. Then she said, 'She's not coming home, she's dead.'

"Just like that. *'She's not coming home, she's dead.'* And that's how I learned that Peggy had died. And now I'm sixty years old and I still have no idea how my sister died. No one ever told me. So when Dad told me that you've been going to Pennsylvania to talk with people about Peggy, I thought, I'm going to tell Don to go to the Grandview Hospital and ask for Peggy's records there. And her death certificate. I already called the hospital and they won't release the records to me. But you can get them."

Over the next two weeks I told Colleen many times about what I had realized on the beach that day with Jack: From the beginning I thought that I was setting out to discover who my mother was in this world. But now I knew that I was also going to discover my father. Muriel was right; from the moment my father lost Peggy, he was cast into some new person, never again to be the person he was during the ten months he spent with my mother. I wanted to know my father as my mother had known him when she fell in love with him, she the prettiest girl anyone in Hatfield could remember, and he a skinny, poor kid who grew up with no plumbing and already had false teeth by the time he met her in 1948. I wanted to know what she had loved about him and seen in him, and it seemed entirely possible to me that it was something he had never again possessed after her death. Something she had taken with her.

Our lives proceed in one direction for so long and then we take a half turn in another direction and the whole purpose of our lives is suddenly out there in front of us. I believe this now. I believe we are even given glimpses of our destiny. And on the cold winter afternoon when I sat with Muriel, Peggy's aunt, I felt for the first time in my life that my destiny was to know my mother. The events of Peggy's life were easy to trace, in part because hers was such a short life and it was lived at a time when things were less complicated than they are today, or if not less complicated, then at least less hurried. For example, a girl who worked with Peggy at the telephone company had no difficulty remembering how Peggy described her first date because a first date in 1948 was just a restaurant meal with a young man. A few hours of conversation and then a memory of that evening which contained no secrets.

I laid down the events of my mother's life along a time line. But the events of our lives do not necessarily convey who we are in this world, and in order for me to connect these events so that they revealed the motives that had inspired them, I had to know the emotions beneath them. I am talking about the only way on earth that anyone ever comes to truly know us. By knowing our fears and our desires, the things that are deep and individual in each of us and the things we try hardest to conceal.

Peggy was an intensely private person who took great measures to conceal these things from the people closest to her. And if she had not opened herself to Muriel, I would only have been able to skate across the surface of her days on this earth. I will always remember and be thankful for Muriel's words to me that winter afternoon: *"Let me tell you who your mother was in this world."* Not only what she did, but how she felt about herself and the life that encircled her.

Muriel's gift to me was inestimable. Without it I would have been left to *imagine* Peggy's feelings. And I might have been wrong as often as I was right. This would not have been good enough. I wanted to *know* my mother. I wanted to know what she was afraid of and what she desired. I wanted to know the precise measurements of her love for my father so that I could give him back his love story in its true shape and texture.

We are living at a time now when we want to know what is true. In the stories that we read, we want to know what actually happened and what was invented. I don't know why exactly. But in this story of mine, invention was not good enough for me. I had no wish to invent my mother, but to reinstate her.

Chapter Ten

Maybe our adult lives begin when we have that first sense that others are oblivious to *our* dreams and *our* desires. Peggy was seventeen when this happened. Later she suspected that it had happened much sooner for her girlfriends; she believed she was late with everything. The season helped— spring itself was a feast to her senses, and that spring of 1948 she could feel the texture of spring for the first time. The way the light struck the cold marble front of the Hatfield Building and Loan on Broad Street. The green grass at the Montgomery County fairgrounds. She was the kind of young girl who walked her own road alone, and she would have felt as if she was taking in the world around her that spring while everyone else was just moving past it, oblivious to the color and the light as well as to how these things registered inside her. I know that she was confused and unsure how this made her feel; on the one hand it gave her an intense and pleasant feeling of freedom and privacy. And on the other hand it made her feel lonely. Even isolated.

That spring of 1948, Peggy awakens early every morning. Long before the first light of dawn she opens her eyes and listens for the sounds of the world which in those days were the whistle of the Philadelphia train running east toward the city and the newspaper delivery truck pulling to the curb in front of I. C. Detweiler's General Store. She plays a game with herself: if she awakens before anyone else, then she can lay claim to the world beyond the walls and roof of this house which contain her. Her father's house. The train whistle starts her heart. The delivery truck fills her lungs with air.

Every few nights she will rearrange the furniture in her room—the twin bed, the bureau, the bedside table, the stuffed chair. She will move these things at night when the room is dark. Then when she opens her eyes in the morning, she will be somewhere else. *Someone else.*

Out of necessity she has been waking up earlier and earlier in order to beat her grandfather who has recently moved in with her to convalesce from a fall he took off a carpenter's scaffold.

In her room she dresses in darkness. Her flannel nightgown she folds in tissue paper and slips into her drawer, a small act to purify the day. And before she leaves the room she kneels down on the floor of her closet to make sure that none of her shoes is out of place. She places her hand on the back of each shoe and pushes so all the toes are lined up against the baseboard. This small gesture folds into the smooth contours of an ordered life and holds together the symmetry of the world. She can sense this and it calms her. At this hour of the morning, the world, to her, is still a fine painting that she will only make a mess of, marching back and forth across it with paint on the soles of her shoes as the day goes on. That is how she thinks of herself in those days. Ungainly and unsure of herself. Not smart enough. Not pretty enough.

In the hallway she stops at the doorway of her brother's room. Jack is ten years old. She has bought him a cowboy's six-shooter and holster for his birthday and it hangs off the bedpost. She listens to him breathing. Sometime in the last year while she was growing into her beauty, the sharp angles of her body giving way to roundness, she had begun seeing her brother as more than a pest who plagued her, hiding her lipstick in the mailbox on the front porch, her underwear in the glove compartment of her father's Ford. She had begun to see him as a person who would go on and take his place in the world, and this as much as any other change seemed to indicate that she had finally left behind her girlhood, ducking below the last breaking waves of adolescence, then emerging as a young woman while the turmoil and confusion washed away beneath her feet.

In a bed across from her brother, Aunt Sue is snoring faintly. She works as a nurse in Philadelphia and visits frequently. Her sister, Lilly, lives three doors away and lately has been giving Peggy a course in advanced sewing. Tonight, in front of both these aunts, Peggy will take her place at the Singer machine with the black wrought-iron legs and the little white light glowing beneath its tin shade.

A few steps away she pauses at the door of her mother and father's bedroom. She can smell the printer's ink on the clothes that her father has left on a chair. Tan khakis, top and bottom. A black leather belt. A white T-shirt. In another hour her mother will awaken to go to work in the cafeteria of the Consolidated School. She will put on her white uniform and the hair net that always makes Peggy feel sorry for her because with the hair net on, her mother doesn't look like herself but like a kitchen worker complying with someone's rules. The hair net, something so light that it is almost weightless in her hand, steals her mother from her and Peggy will turn away whenever her mother puts it on in her presence.

In the kitchen on these early mornings, Peggy's grandfather is already sitting at the oak table, his head in his hands. Something is knocked down inside her when she sees that he has beaten her to the day.

She waits for him to finish his silent morning prayers, then touches his shoulder. Here is a man who dropped thirty feet from a carpenter's scaffolding and landed on his back, the scaffold planks and all his tools crashing down on top of him. When the doctor examined him in the emergency room at Grandview Hospital in Sellersville he exclaimed, "You're in so many pieces, Howard, that I don't know where to start." He's an early riser out of habit, a carpenter who always prided himself on being the first one at George Snyder's lumberyard each day to pick up his stock. He is an old man with a head of white waves, but his body is as hard as wood. "You have to be strong in this life, Peggy," he has always told her. It is his battle cry and whenever he says it, it makes Peggy wonder just how strong she is, and will have to be.

He wants to show her what he has made with his big square hands. He is very pleased with himself when he takes it from the vise that he has screwed to the kitchen table so the glue would dry overnight. It's a kind of wedge that he has carved out of wood and attached to the sole of his right shoe to compensate for the leg that has withered since his accident. The doctor had wanted to amputate the leg, but he healed it on his own, though it has shrunk three inches now. "How do you like it, what do you think?" he asks Peggy.

He wants to try it on and give it a test right now. She watches him walk to the sink and back, clomping like a horse. It is Peggy's idea to put it to the real test. A few dance steps— not a slow dance, but the jitterbug.

"The jitterbug?" he asks.

"You have to be strong in this life!" she tells him with her green eyes brightening.

He is whirling her around, smiling back with pride. She has a new move, a little slide step that she has been rehearsing in her room with the door closed. When she shows him, he raises his eyebrows appreciatively. It makes her feel lucky to have been born at a time when the deep, driving bass notes of the dance music of America match so completely the rhythms of her heart.

She lays some coal in the cookstove and makes oatmeal for the two of them. "No cream," she tells him, "only skim milk."

"You could afford to put on a little weight. You'll dance it off anyway at the rate you're going these days. Out every night. Do you ever dance with the same boy twice?"

"Haven't found one yet who can keep up with me. Now eat your oatmeal and stop snooping."

She thinks of him now, the boy she met last Friday night at Sunnybrook in Pottstown. Who's the skinny guy with the angel? she'd overheard someone ask. *The skinny guy and the angel* . . . She smiles to herself as she thinks about how he kept hitching up his flannel trousers. Maybe they fit him before he went to the war. From the big bay window in the dance hall he pointed out his new Chevy.

"It's the convertible," he said with pleasure. "The green one over there."

It was too dark to see but she told him it looked like a fine automobile.

She had one dance and one glass of punch in cut crystal cups. He offered her a cigarette which she declined.

"So, what do you do with yourself?" he asked her.

She told him that she was working at the telephone company in Lansdale, saving her money to move somewhere.

"Move somewhere?"

"Maybe to a big city like New York."

A sad look passed over his face, and she would have taken note of this.

But he recovered quickly and said he didn't know why anyone would want to leave this part of Pennsylvania. He was so glad to be back after two years in the army. The first thing he had done when he got home was drive up and down every street in Skippack, where he'd been a boy. Down the streets where he used to deliver newspapers on his bicycle.

He paused then and Peggy thought he had gone down all the old streets to see how things had changed since he'd left for the war.

And what he said next was what she would remember to tell her aunt. He had looked right into her eyes with his lit-up smile and said, "Mostly, I guess I did it to see how *I'd* changed."

Later that spring she overhears one of the girls at the telephone company telling someone about a man on the Cowpath Road in Lansdale who is building a bomb shelter in his backyard. One afternoon, rather than take the trolley home from work, she rides along with her friend so she can see firsthand.

They park a few blocks away then walk across the street, their heels clacking on the hard macadam road, reminding Peggy that she had spent too much of her first paycheck buying these heels at Stuart's shoe store. All the girls were wearing them now, even to jitterbug in, and they make her feel tall and elegant, but she is still kicking herself for succumbing to the fashion when what she really wanted to do was put the money into her savings account so that one day she could go clacking down the busy streets of some distant city where no one would know her and where she would be free to do whatever she liked, including spending a whole day just staring out a window, barely moving, just watching people go by in their busy lives. This kind of blessed anonymity she has only felt twice in her life, both times when she went to the Allentown fair and allowed herself the rare pleasure of disappearing into the throngs of people who swept her along in their momentum.

It had been exhilarating, but if she heeds the polio warnings she will miss the fair this summer. The thought of missing it, of missing the chance to disappear from herself for a few hours and to feel the velocity of life in the people around her, is as much a threat to her as the thought of polio condemning her to a lifetime of metal braces the way it had poor Frances Snyder, whose father owned the Atlantic station on Main Street, a girl exactly Peggy's age who, they said, would never walk again.

From the curb the two of them can see mounds of dirt in the backyard of a small one-story house.

"I bet it's only a swimming pool," her friend says.

Peggy wants to laugh along with her, but she can't because her grandfather has already told her that the bomb shelter would be finished off with reinforced concrete. The only way in and out will be a round hole in the top with a concrete lid that screws on.

Peggy doesn't want to make a big deal out of this but while her friend is speaking, a fear spreads through her. All Peggy can think about is the houses of her friends, and the dance hall in Pottstown and the Consolidated School and the movie theaters in Lansdale being blown to smithereens. During the war she used to stand outside with her father at night, keeping watch for enemy airplanes. Her father had a chart that showed the silhouettes of every enemy airplane. He would bring the chart with him each time. She will always remember how he would lean back on his heels and look up at the sky, his suspenders buckling a little on his shoulders. "When it happens," he had said to her once, "they won't be airplanes, they'll be rockets coming over from Russia. You'll look up into the sky and they'll be like these great huge cigars crossing from the horizon and that'll be the end of everything!"

The air will be full of flying glass, her father told her, and everything will stop.

Her friend is speaking again, telling her that if there is going to be a war with the Russians, the thing that will make her maddest of all is that she never *did* anything.

"You know what I mean, Peg? *With a boy?* Always afraid that somebody would think we were bad girls."

Peggy keeps looking at the torn-up earth and wonders what kind of man builds a bomb shelter in his backyard anyway. How frightened would a man have to be? Perhaps he was in the last war and he saw something that he never wants to see again.

"Did you hear what I said, Peg? We were too young when the boys left for the war, too young to say goodbye properly. And when they came home we were *too good* to properly say hello."

Peggy can hear her but she doesn't answer; this has been going on for some time now, the sounds of the real world failing to reach her. Failing to penetrate her thoughts. Her deep thoughts. A teacher in her last year of high school told her that she was a girl who hid *inside* her thoughts and *behind* her beauty. At the time Peggy wanted to deny this, but couldn't. It has grown worse; at work lately she drifts away without warning, sometimes right in the middle of placing a call. In a room filled with voices and the blinking lights of the switchboards she is able to just vanish.

Aloof. That is the word one friend accused her of. She's too pretty and too independent for the rest of the world. So she acts aloof.

But she does not feel aloof. She feels inadequate and temporary. Maybe it was the war that had made her feel this way. Or maybe it was just the fear that ran so deep in her, the fear that she might live her whole life waiting for her life to start. This was something she often thought about during the war. How people's lives ended before they had begun. So many of the soldiers were boys really, young and innocent. And the children killed in the bombed-out cities, not just the children on our side, but the Japanese and German children as well. At work there had been talk about the boy from Lansdale who was killed in France. Peggy had wondered at the time if a beautiful French girl with rouge on her cheeks had kissed him before he was killed. She wondered if God forgives the girls who make love to the soldiers that go on to die in war. If God looks upon this as an act of benevolence.

They stop at Inky's ice cream parlor for a cone on the way home. Strawberry for Peggy and even as she is eating it she is planning to take a long ride on her bicycle when she gets home to work off the calories. The diner is packed with high school kids. They all look so sure of themselves to her: Where do they get their self-confidence? Some of the girls, in an act of teenage rebellion, have traded one of their bobby socks and one saddle shoe for a sock and shoe that don't match. As self-assured and full of themselves as they appear to be, she still wouldn't want to trade places with these girls; high school had been an endless repetition of long days spent trying to take hold of something meaningful, *anything* that would amount to something more than just words delivered by teachers who had forgotten long ago what it was like to be young, to be desperate to join the real world beyond the classroom walls and windows.

In a corner booth a baby has begun to cry and immediately Peggy and her friend are rising from their seats to get a look. Her friend says, Have you noticed that there are babies positively everywhere lately? Gosh, I want one, don't you, Peggy?

Someday, maybe, she replies. There were other things she wanted to do first, and though she couldn't name these things precisely, they belonged to an imagined life that was different from her mother's life of cooking and cleaning up after a family. She hopes to venture far from that kind of hemmed-in life, but in the diner, when the young mother stills her baby's cries, it is a marvelous thing to observe. The baby, sitting on her mother's arm like a puppet, is suddenly smiling and looking around the room with a bright and knowing expression.

How exquisite to be so good at something, to possess a heart that is capable of consoling another human being. This is something real and meaningful in a world of abstractions and uncertainties. A world that Peggy so seldom feels a part of. A world that was proclaiming its heartache in tonight's newspaper headlines that told how the Russian army had begun entrenching along the 38th parallel in Korea. Picture them! *A whole army of men digging holes!* An interminable line of men in uniform bent over shovels on the other side of the world. And on this side another army of young husbands digging up their backyards to make room for bomb shelters with concrete lids that screw shut. What a strange world it was, so difficult to get inside of. At one moment its heartache was distant and immeasurable, and in the next it was there, right in front of Peggy, on the streets of her small town. Down along Broad Street, past the school yard where the swings move slightly in the soft wind, there is the Wimmer house, the little brick house with the gable above the front door and the flag with its single star in the front window. In the lighted living room on any night, people sit in front of the radio. The war has been over for three years now. The son who used to *live* in this *living room* has been dead for almost four years. The people in this room once waited for him to write to them from the war, and then they waited for his body to be returned from France. Now life is going on without him. The patterns of a day are once again holding together despite the awful loss. This is one of the things that are difficult to make sense of. Isn't this the *definition* of sadness to a young girl like Peggy? The way that life goes on after a loved one is lost seems to be almost as sad as the loss itself.

BOOK TWO

Chapter Eleven

The Grandview Hospital, Sellersville, Pennsylvania. Room 9. A man with a purple face is sleeping on one bed. The other bed is empty. I joke with a nurse that when my generation is old there won't be an empty bed in any hospital in America. "I'll leave you alone," she whispers.

I see the two large windows that my mother was looking out of when she died on August 27, 1950. Today they are streaked with rain but on a sunny August afternoon they would have showed Peggy green hills, farms and silos, the highway running back home, back to everything that she had known and trusted in her life and believed she would be a part of for a very long time. From this room she could have seen a long, long way.

The hospital records begin with this account:

16 days ago, patient was delivered of twins. The delivery was preceded by toxemia of pregnancy which was manifested by swelling of face and legs, elevation of blood pressure and albumin in the urine. She went into spontaneous labor and twins were extracted by low forcep application. The obstetrician, Dr. Edward Wright, stated she did not have excessive bleeding but several days post partum was

given 1 quart of blood and on discharge from the hospital she was said to have 47% hemoglobin and RBC of 3,000. She did not improve at home and was admitted to this hospital at 3:19 p.m. on August 27.

19 yr. old female routinely admitted to S.P. #9, brought via Lansdale ambulance. Sent in by Dr. P. T. Moyer to be under medical service of Dr. Peters. Pt. looks very pale and tired. Slight vaginal bleeding. B.P. 166/90.

4 p.m. request for blood work sent to lab. stat.

4:09 p.m. visited by Dr. Peters.

4:30 p.m. 500cc w. c. blood started I.V. by Dr. Peters—running very well—

4:45 p.m. pt. [patient] complaining of "queer feeling in head" "feels hot all over"—blood stopped. Dr. Peters called—respiration becoming extremely labored.

4:48 Caff.Sod.Benz. GR 7½ IV. given by Dr. Peters.

4:50 Patient not responsive—R.H.S. pronounced dead by Dr. Peters.

I am reading these notations for the fifth time when the man with the purple face awakens and looks at me.

Dr. P. T. Moyer is dead. Dr. Peters is dead. Dr. Wright is dead.

"Everyone is dead," I tell the man with the purple face. "I waited too long."

He looks at me with bloodshot eyes. I believe that my mumbling has frightened him. I tell him I am sorry and make my way home.

. . .

Tom Pugles never heard the story of his sister's sleepover
when the girls rode in his father's truck to pick up fruits and
vegetables for his market. When I recount this story, it brings
a light to his eyes. We are sitting at a square table in Zoto's
Diner in Line Lexington and he is telling me about the trip to
Canada that he and my father took together after the war,
before my father met Peggy. It was a vacation for both of
them. They drove in my father's green Chevrolet convertible.
They were carefree days, the two of them best friends, sleeping out at night under the stars.

He has a photograph he took of my father when they
stopped for a night in Bar Harbor, Maine. In front of a shoe
store my father is standing in a pair of enormous shoes, size
sixteen or seventeen. He is looking down at his feet and
laughing.

Tom's sister, Lorraine, has written me from Florida to tell
me about the days when my father was dating her. She was his
first date after he returned home from the war. "He was very
romantic," she has written. "He wrote me letters after each
date." On one date they took a picnic supper to the Jersey
shore. They stayed late after everyone else had left the beach.
My father climbed up into the lifeguard stand and gave a
Tarzan yell.

There is another photograph, of my father and Tom and
two young women at Greenlake Park where they had gone for
my father's twenty-first birthday. Tom is laughing in the photograph as my father sneaks behind one of the girls and puts
up two fingers behind her head.

I have no memories of my father as a carefree man. He was
always kind, but never carefree. I remember when we lived on

Clearspring Road he had a push lawn mower and I would walk beside him as he mowed the grass. He always mowed from right to left and I walked along beside him, to his right, in the lane he had just made with the mower. There was only the clicking of the blades as they spun through the grass. I would ask him questions and he would answer me, but our conversation quickly lapsed into silent stretches that he never broke. I remember vividly how, on one occasion, he explained to me what a "perfect game" was in baseball.

Then he bought a power mower, and the gasoline engine made too much noise for dialogue. I still walked beside him. I remember seeing his lips move sometimes, and I realized that he was talking to himself as the power mower pulled him along.

Tom Pugles and I are the last to leave the diner. A young waitress is wiping off the tables around us when Tom tells me that after Peggy's death my father confided to him that he was going to kill himself by driving onto the railroad tracks on Broad Street in Lansdale, in front of the express train from Philadelphia. In the weeks after Peggy's death, Tom would sit up all night with my father, drinking coffee and smoking Salem cigarettes. Tom was working as a state trooper in those days. He wanted me to know about one night in particular. He had gone straight to my father's apartment without taking the time to change out of his uniform. When he was walking to the front door he saw my father running from window to window, locking them, and then the front door. "Your father was convinced that I had come to arrest him and put him in jail for Peggy's death," he tells me.

That night Tom had stood outside the front door calling to my father until he finally opened the door. Then he carefully explained to him that he had not killed Peggy. A few nights later Tom didn't have time to change out of his uniform before he went to visit my father, and the same thing happened again. In his sadness my father seemed to have lost his mind.

I am sinking into the horror of this image of my father, and the words on my mother's hospital record. . . .

It is all becoming very real to me for the first time in my life. I can see the waitress standing behind Tom, waiting for us to get up so she can clear our table. Tom is talking about my father before Peggy's death, his great optimism, his smile, and the way he could dance the jitterbug. People always loved to see Dick Snyder coming in their direction. Never a mean thing to say about anyone. Always forgiving.

I am listening but I see him locking the door, running from window to window, locking them as well. Each day a small steady decline into a depthless, all-consuming sorrow.

I don't remember getting up from the table that night, or leaving the diner, or driving home.

Chapter Twelve

Under the headline "SON WRITES PARENTS' LOVE STORY," *The Reporter,* a daily newspaper for the Hatfield, Pennsylvania, area, ran a front-page story with the photograph of my mother and father in the wedding car. The article requested that anyone who had known Peggy write or call me in Maine.

There were many letters; new ones arrived every morning in the day's mail:

> I remember as if it was just the other day, I was standing on my front porch with my best girlfriend when the funeral procession went past. It came to me at once that this must be the funeral of the dear young mother of the twin boys . . . For all these years I have wondered what ever became of these boys. Saturday when I picked up the newspaper, I finally knew.
>
> I'll never forget the utterly devastated, traumatized, grieving broken man who visited me to tell me his young wife had died, leaving newborn baby boys. It is hard enough to write about it even now, let alone talk about it through the years. I think it was a traumatic experience for everyone in the town

of Hatfield. He kept repeating, "I didn't know . . . No one told me." Now at this time I don't know whether he meant that no one told him just how ill she was . . . My heart ached for him and I wanted to say I would be glad to care for the babies (even with no previous experience).

For the fifty-seven years that I lived in Hatfield (on Cherry Street) I never remember anything so sad as the death of Peggy Schwartz. Many people like myself found it hard to pick our heads up and go on after that. But of course you must go on.

I have read that you are writing the story of your mother, Peggy Schwartz Snyder. I want you to know that I, too, was pregnant with twins in the same year as Peggy. We had the same doctor. Dr. Wright. He was an exceptional doctor, a tall, handsome man with bright eyes. Very intelligent and thorough. I had such extreme toxemia starting in the third month of my pregnancy that the doctor told me if things continued this toxemia would become preeclampsia and he would have to take my babies early, probably in the sixth month at the latest. I got worse and worse and in my twenty-sixth week, my babies were taken. They were twin boys like you and your brother. They only lived one day . . . In those days babies taken or born early before their lungs were developed could not live. Your mother must have been very brave to carry you and your brother through her full term.

Jack Schwartz, my uncle, had no idea about these letters or what people were writing me about my mother's death. These words "eclampsia," "toxemia," strange words to me then, words I had never heard before in any of Colleen's pregnancies, were adding up to something that I failed to recognize even when Jack called from his home in Vermont to tell me about an article he had just run across in a magazine. "I think I finally know what killed Peggy," he said on the telephone.

In the January 1998 issue of *Worth* magazine there was a story under the title "The Best Medicine . . . The AMA doesn't think ordinary Americans can handle the truth about their doctors. Tell that to what's left of the Grossman family."

The story was about a young pregnant woman who died of eclampsia in 1986. Eclampsia, described as extreme toxemia, killed the woman despite attentive care by her physician, and the additional scrutiny of her own father who was also a physician. The diagnosis, so simple to confirm by taking a patient's blood pressure, is also equally simple to miss. In this story the woman's normal baseline blood pressure was particularly low, and so her blood pressure during pregnancy, which did not appear dangerously high to her physician, *was*.

"I read the article and the whole time I was reading it, something said to me, this is what killed Peggy. I'm probably wrong. But I'm sending you the article anyway," Jack said.

One of the most helpful letters I received was from an eighty-seven-year-old woman in a nursing home who told me about Anna Hartman, who was the labor and delivery nurse at the Elm Terrace Hospital for thirty-two years. She sent me a newspaper article that had appeared when Mrs. Hartman retired; it contained a thorough description of the Elm Terrace Hospital at the time my mother was a maternity patient there. I wrote her a letter thanking her, and she replied immediately that someone she knew had recently told her that Anna Hartman was still alive. She was going to try to contact her, and she asked me to call her after a few days if I wanted to speak with Anna Hartman about my mother.

That night I dreamed that I was standing in front of the Elm Terrace Hospital. It was summer and the tall shade trees on the lawn were blowing in a warm wind. On the porch, pregnant girls were sitting in white wicker rocking chairs. I could see inside the front door, a tall heavy door like the door of a church, and beyond into the foyer with the dark scrolled banister and the oak staircase where two men were carrying a woman on a stretcher up to the delivery room on the second floor. She was crying out for someone to help her and I was calling to the pregnant girls in their white wicker chairs on the porch, asking who was on the stretcher, but they couldn't hear me. I ran down Broad Street to the corner of Fourth to Dr. Wright's office in the big Victorian house with white crown molding and gables covered in vines. All the lights were off. But there was a man sitting on the front steps. He was holding something in his hand, gesturing for me to take it. In the light of a streetlamp I could see that he had handed me the medical records from the Grandview Hospital where Peggy died. I read the lines again ". . . 4:45 p.m. pt. complaining of 'queer feeling in head' 'feels hot all over'—blood stopped. Dr. Peters called—respiration becoming extremely labored. 4:48 Caff.Sod.Benz. GR 7½ IV. given by Dr. Peters. 4:50 Patient not responsive—R.H.S. pronounced dead by Dr. Peters." I ran back down the street to the Elm Terrace Hospital and began telling the pregnant girls that there had been some mistake, that Peggy Snyder couldn't be dead because she was on the stretcher, being carried up the stairs to have her babies. The pregnant girls had their heads bowed. The wicker rocking chairs were still, and the pregnant girls were asleep. I stepped closer to the porch and saw that one of the sleeping girls was Erin, my twelve-year-old daughter, grown up. Her eyes were closed but there were tears running down her cheeks.

I awoke from this dream and went straight to Erin's room. Her white down comforter had fallen from her bed. When I covered her I thought about how I used to lift her from her crib in the middle of the night to carry her back into my bed so Colleen could feed her. I would wrap her tightly in a small blanket, her arms against her sides inside the blanket. Colleen would turn onto one side, unbutton her nightgown, and place her nipple to Erin's lips. Those days of my daughter's infancy were the unhurried days of my own love story with Colleen, when the three of us would lie in bed all afternoon, enclosed within a tenderness for one another that the world could not diminish.

I looked down at Erin, her long legs beneath the blanket, so improbably long to me. She was coming into her own now, taking voice lessons, auditioning for parts in a children's theater. She would march into the living room on a Sunday afternoon where her brother and I were camped out on the couch watching one football game turn into another and she'd let us have it: "I can't believe you're going to just lie there watching dumb football games all day!"

I have also seen this daughter with a far-off look in her eyes, and I've wondered if she inherited from my mother the same deep, perplexing loneliness that has always been the strongest emotion in me, stronger than love, anger, or ambition, a feeling so persistent that it could convince you in a moment it was a loneliness you had earned and would carry with you because you were worthy of nothing else.

My mother had created me and then re-created herself in my daughter. Tonight, looking down at her in her bed, I wondered how much of my mother she carried inside her. How much of who she was becoming had been shaped by a person she would never know. I went downstairs and took Erin's baby journal off the bookshelf next to the fireplace. I began reading the pages, searching for the places where I had written to her about Peggy. I read about her first Christmas, her first day of school, the day she learned to ride a bicycle, the afternoon I buried her dog. But there was nothing about Peggy and now there was no room left to write anything.

Chapter Thirteen

My mother's closest friends from high school have met me at the Heritage Hotel outside Collegeville to tell me about her. Adelle, who played field hockey with Peggy for two years in high school and walked home with her every night from practice. Adelle graduated first in the class, went on to Ursinus College, and learned to fly an airplane. Peg, who was a nursing student at Grandview. She was on duty on the third floor of the hospital on Sunday afternoon, August 27, 1950, but did not find out until the next day that my mother, her dearest friend, had died in semiprivate room 9, one floor below her. Julia, who had met my father before she became friends with Peggy because she was a close friend of my father's cousin Frances, who was paralyzed from polio. And Ginny, who threw an engagement party for Peggy in her basement and for years after her death went to visit my grandmother and grandfather every Sunday afternoon. "First," she said, "because I needed to, and then after a while because it had become a habit."

Adelle remembered coming home from college for Christmas and going to see Peggy in the apartment on North Broad Street in Lansdale. It was only a month after Peggy and my father were married, and Adelle asked her what her husband was going to get her for Christmas. "I'm giving Dick big hints," Peggy told her. "I pretend to be talking in my sleep, saying, 'Pearls, pearls, pearls.'"

I listened to these ladies as they laughed about their high school senior trip to Washington, D.C., and my mother's brief romance with a man who placed bets over the telephone when she was working at the telephone company.

Peg stayed for a while after the other ladies had said goodbye. She spoke at length about my mother and then, with tears in her eyes, she handed me an envelope. "I want you to have this," she said.

It was a pale green envelope addressed:

Miss Peggy Kirsch
Nurses Home
Grand View Hospital
Sellersville, Penna

The postmark was January 11, 1950, 9:30 a.m.

There was a three-cent stamp in the upper right-hand corner. The *P*s in *Peggy* and *Penna* were fat and rounded, as if they had been written by a small child still thrilled by her newly acquired ability to write in cursive.

Printed on the back of the envelope:

Mrs Richard Snyder
623 North Broad Street
Lansdale, Pa.

My mother's personal stationery. Her new married name was also printed at the top of the enclosed five-by-eight-inch sheet of paper.

In the only letter I would ever have of my mother's she wrote with the same cursive flourishes:

> Dear Peggy,
>
> If this letter is a wee bit sloppy please excuse it, because I'm writing in bed.
>
> Please forgive us for not coming over last week but I was sick every night but one and that night we got company. I thought I had a cold in my stomach, because I was sick in my stomach every day for more than a week, so last Wed. night I went to the Dr. and I told him how I felt and he asked me some questions and guess what he said—he said I was pregnant, isn't that wonderful. I'm going to Scared (not spelled right) Heart in Norristown next September.
>
> Are you surprised? So was I.
>
> Did you have a nice vacation? I hope so.
>
> I don't know what to tell you. I guess I didn't say much, I just wanted you to know I was thinking about you.
>
> Please write to me.
>
> Love,
> Peggy.

My eyes filled with tears before I finished.

"I think I was her first friend she told," Peg said. "It's been so long ago and there's so much that I've forgotten, but when I read the letter I wondered why Peggy says she's going to have her baby in Norristown. She'd already made up her mind in the first month of her pregnancy. Everyone had their babies at Elm Terrace or at Grandview in those days."

I knew what it meant because of the woman who had written to me after the *Reporter* article appeared, the woman who was so sick in her pregnancy that her doctor, Dr. Wright, sent her to Norristown where her life had been saved.

I told Peg about this and I asked her if my mother had ever said anything to her about being sick when she was pregnant.

"Nothing, but that's something else I wanted to tell you. I never saw Peggy once she became pregnant. Neither did any of her other close friends. We never saw her once during the time she was carrying you twins. And I've brought you something else that's a mystery to me."

Another envelope addressed in my mother's handwriting with the distinctive fat, round *P:*

Miss Peg Kirsch
Grand View Hospital
Sellersville, Pa.

It was a tiny envelope two-and-a-half-inches-by-three-inches. Inside was a small card with a child's painting of a baby holding a pink umbrella with a blue ribbon tied to its hooked handle.

You're invited to a
BABY SHOWER
DATE: MAY 22
TIME: 8:00
FOR: PEG SNYDER
PLACE: JENNY EBERHARDT

"Do you remember how my mother seemed at the shower?" I asked Peg.

"I'm sure I never went. And here, look at the date of the postmark."

The envelope was postmarked June 8.

The shower was to take place May 22.

"No one went to her shower because she mailed the invitations two weeks late," Peg said. "She didn't want anyone to see her, I'm sure of it. This was in what would have been the last three months of her pregnancy."

Peg let me keep the invitation and the letter. When we said goodbye we held each other outside the restaurant, in the rain.

"There's a lot that no one knows about your mother," she said to me. "Peggy was very, very private; if she was sick she never would have told anyone, not even your father. *Particularly* not your father. But you have to find out exactly what was going on. Don't stop until you know all that there is to know."

I used a pay phone at the restaurant to call the woman in the nursing home who was going to set up a meeting for me with the Anna Hartman who had been my mother's nurse at the Elm Terrace Hospital during her delivery. My idea was to drive straight from the restaurant to see Anna. She would remember, I was sure, the young mother who died after giving birth to twins. And I hoped she might also be able to tell me what had happened to Peggy, what had caused her to become so sick.

"This is Don Snyder, Peggy Snyder's son," I said when she answered the telephone.

"Oh my," she said. "I called your house in Maine this morning and your wife told me you were here. I'm sorry. Anna Hartman died yesterday."

.   .   .

I drove fast through the rain to Lansdale with my mother's letter to Peg on the seat beside me. It was raining too hard to read the numbers on the apartments on North Broad Street so I rolled the window down and leaned across the seat. When I thought I had found the right place I pulled the car to a stop on the side of the street and ran out into the pouring rain. I could feel the blood pounding in my head. I was asking myself, "What are you doing?" And it was number 632, not 623. Running back down to the sidewalk, I reached inside the car window I had left open and grabbed the letter. The ink on the envelope had begun to bleed from the rain.

I ran down the street and then across, through the traffic, to number 623. It was a brick walk-up, adjoined on both sides by identical apartments. I knocked hard on the front door and peered through the glass in the door to a dark corridor with a doorway on the right. No one answered and I went to the windows lining the front porch, knocking on each of them, knowing that it was no use because there wasn't anyone home, but knocking anyway. I could see a couch through the windows and two chairs. I could picture Peggy walking through these rooms with my father. Some part of me believed that if I stayed there long enough someone would open the door for me and let me walk through the rooms and I would find something that had belonged to my mother, some small thing that would explain why she was planning even in the first month of her pregnancy to have her baby in Norristown instead of the Elm Terrace Hospital which had stood across the street where there was now an apartment building. Even as I was driving away and holding the letter over the car's heater to dry it before my mother's handwriting disappeared, I was thinking that someday I would know why she had not mailed the invitations to her baby shower until two weeks after it was supposed to take place.

I drove to the North Penn Hospital next, the hospital that replaced Elm Terrace. A woman in the office where they keep medical records told me that all records from the old Elm Terrace Hospital had been destroyed. "We have nothing here," she said. "The records are gone."

I was standing at her desk soaking wet from the rain, asking her about something that had happened almost fifty years ago, long before she was born. I realized that I was leaning over her desk, too close to her, and dripping water on her papers. I had this feeling that she thought I was a lunatic who had wandered inside from the storm. I gave her my mother's letter to read. When she was finished I told her that it was the only thing I had that my mother had ever written and that I had to find out what had happened to her. "She was only nineteen years old?" she said after I had told her my story.

"What about her doctor's records?" I asked. "Dr. Wright. Dr. Edward Wright, whose office was on Broad and Third streets?"

"They would have been disposed of by his family when he died," she said. "We wouldn't have anything."

I asked her if she would take my name and telephone number just in case. As she was writing them down she said, "I'm really sorry, sir, but I don't think there's anything I can do to help you."

I found my father sitting at the dining-room table with the telephone and sheets of notebook paper. I stood inside the door and before I had even taken off my boots I was hitting him with questions. "The word 'eclampsia,' Dad—did you ever hear the doctor use that word? How did she die then, Dad? How come no one ever found out how she died! And do you remember the baby shower that she never went to? Here—have you ever seen one of these invitations? And why was she going to have her baby in Norristown? She must have talked with you about this? None of her girlfriends ever saw her when she was pregnant. None of them. What was she hiding from? And your apartment on Broad Street was right across the street from the Elm Terrace Hospital; weren't you there every damned day asking Dr. Wright why she wasn't getting better?"

He looked at me with a puzzled expression. "We weren't living in the apartment on Broad Street, we moved to Grandmother Schwartz's house in Hatfield."

"I know you did. *Why?*"

"So Grandmother could help out."

"Help out with what, Dad? You were living there with Peggy and her mother and father and brother and her grandparents, and God knows, maybe two aunts—all of you crammed into that tiny half of a house, and no one could see that Peggy was dying? No one could pick up the damned telephone and call the doctor? I don't get it . . . I don't understand how she could get worse every day from the day we were born—"

"On August eleventh," he said helplessly.

"Right, August eleventh. And they send her home from the hospital on the twentieth and she can't walk on her own—that's what Peg Kirsch told me she had been told. And she'd stopped eating completely. And it goes on for seven more days and no one calls Dr. Wright and tells him to do something? You're going to have to help me figure this out, Dad, because I'm sorry, but I just don't get it."

I put my boots back on and went outside and smoked a cigarette. When I came back, my father was still at the table. He picked up a piece of paper and said, "I wrote down the names of all Peggy's bridesmaids at the wedding."

I took a deep breath.

"I called one of the girls and told her that you were writing Peggy's memoirs. She wants to talk to you."

I took the piece of paper.

"I just wanted to help you, Donnie," he said to me. "I wish I could remember all these things."

It was all out of me. I told him I was sorry.

Chapter Fourteen

Of all things, Peggy's first real fling is with a bookie from Camden, New Jersey. It begins in the heat of July, in the summer of 1948. Actually he sends her a dozen peach-colored roses in May and a wide-brimmed straw hat in June with the same peach-color ribbon around the brim, both of these offerings because he found her voice so pleasant when she helped him take his bets through the switchboard of the telephone company in Lansdale. Some of the girls at work have teased her about this secret admirer, making him out to be a rogue like Rhett Butler in *Gone With the Wind.* He bets on everything, it seems: professional baseball games in both the big leagues and the minor leagues; the women's field hockey world championships which interested Peggy a great deal; the Wednesday-night fights which she found herself listening to on the radio lately, much to the puzzlement of her father who always sat in the stuffed chair listening by himself.

In July the summer Olympic games begin at Wembley Park in England after a lapse of twelve years, and the bookie has drawn her into the excitement surrounding the performance of a Dutch housewife named Fanny Blankers. The thirty-year-old mother of two from Amsterdam has won three gold medals in the hurdles and sprints and the bookie claims to have made a thousand dollars by betting on her.

He makes Peggy a simple proposition: if Fanny captures a fourth gold medal, then she must meet him in Souderton for dinner.

There is something about his voice that makes this offer attractive. Something wise and worldly. There is also the satisfaction of knowing how out of sorts her father would be to know that she had accepted a blind date from a bookie! Lately she has been searching for ways to threaten the principles he is so determined to stand upon. Her sweaters are too tight. She is spending too much time alone in her room. She disappears just when everyone else in the house is sitting down to meals. The dance moves that she rehearses upstairs rattle the pictures on the walls downstairs. And she refuses to date anyone, preferring instead to go out in large packs of girls and boys and then answering his queries about what she'd been doing and where she'd gone with the same vague answer each time he waits up for her: We were messing around, that's all.

Messing around?

Messing around, that's all.

So the Dutch housewife wins her fourth gold medal and Peggy takes the commuter train to Souderton on a Saturday night. She angers her father by wearing jeans rolled up to her knees and a cotton shirt with the tails hanging out, partly to provoke him and partly as a precaution because she has told the bookie that she will be wearing a green sundress; this way she can stand him up at the last minute if he shows up the way one of the girls at work predicted he would, sporting a thin moustache and wearing a zoot suit.

Actually he is dressed rather like a Fuller Brush salesman. A stiff blue suit with a white carnation in his lapel. He has jet black hair ironed straight back from his forehead above his pale gray eyes. He is carrying a newspaper rolled up like a telescope, which he is tapping against his thigh as he looks around the restaurant. As the diners turn to regard him he gives them each a pleasant half smile and a nod.

Friendly enough, Peggy guesses. So she raises her hand. He walks toward her with quick precise steps, which could be what remains of a march from his war days or which might indicate his eagerness.

They shake hands. His name is Robert Marsh. He calls her Miss Schwartz and tells her to call him Robert.

So, Mr. Marsh, she says. How much money have you made on your bets today?

He unfolds the newspaper and shows her the box scores of last night's ball games. Two dollars here. Three-fifty here.

Do you ever lose, Mr. Marsh?

I could lose tonight, he tells her with a shy expression, placing his elbows on the Formica table, making a little pedestal of his hands and resting his chin on his knuckles.

What is it you're betting on tonight? she asks, though she is aware that she's walking straight into his trap.

I'm betting you'll let me kiss you when I take you home.

The room seems to fall to silence around her.

She leans back in her chair, crossing her arms in front of her.

How much have you wagered, Mr. Marsh?

A great deal. My life's savings.

Maybe I'll let you win if you agree to split the jackpot with me.

He puts out his hand for her to shake. Deal, he says.

On the finger where a wedding ring would be, he is wearing a gold ring with the University of Virginia embossed on its face.

She shakes his hand.

What is interesting about him is that all through dinner he only asks her about herself and her life. She has scarcely been in the presence of a boy before who didn't go on and on about himself.

But this is hardly a boy. Late twenties, nearly thirty years old, she guesses.

And the war? she says finally. Where did you spend the war?

Italy. In a tank division. Chasing around Mussolini. It was boring most of the time, and terrifying the rest. But I did manage to get to Venice. I went to the grave of John Keats and found that visitors had left notes on his headstone. They had written of their own difficulties in life as though they expected that there would be a response. As if seeking the counsel of God himself. I found it very strange. And touching. Do you know the poetry of John Keats, Miss Schwartz?

The poetry of John Keats. He might just as well have asked her to describe a street in Paris. Any question that exposed the vastness of what she didn't know was a small terror that caused Peggy to withdraw into herself, back to the secret place where she drew comfort from lining up the shoes in her closet and wrapping her clothing neatly in tissue paper, and locking the front door of the house then making herself walk back downstairs to check and see if she locked it. Those crazy acts to purify the day, if performed diligently, can keep the world from ever finding out that she is not worthy of taking up space and air.

But sometimes they are not enough. There is so much in the world that she doesn't know and will never know, and she might hide behind her beauty and her thoughts, concealing from some people her ignorance and her unworthiness, but not from everyone. Not from the people who get too close to her.

Even if the bookie smiles a little half smile meant to reassure this pretty girl, is it enough to keep her from drifting away from this table and this restaurant and his presence? He isn't the first person to try to win her back from herself, to try to call to her before she disappears in a place she would never describe to anyone, a place that might have felt to her like the smooth walls of a vault rising up around her, imprisoning her in a blackness that she cannot climb out of. Like the walls of a bomb shelter, so smooth and so high that they keep her from ever imagining herself as competent as the Dutch housewife winning Olympic medals or as intelligent as this man who understands the poetry of the world. Walls and a cement lid threaded like a bolt that screws down above her.

Chapter Fifteen

And so, through the long summer she is always returning
from that dark vault which contains her and surrounds
her with the terrifying knowledge of her own unworthiness.

You'd better change your attitude, her father tells her.

Where are you, Peggy? her mother asks again and again.

How could she answer her mother's question? Would the
question only add to her darkness? Would the distance separating her from these people she loved push her so far into
darkness that she tried desperately to force her mind to concentrate upon what she knew to be true and familiar, like the
little town of Hatfield? A picture in her mind that might
release her from the terrible darkness? A picture of the Town
Center where she lives in the real world. The loading platform behind the lumberyard and the holding pens for sheep
and cattle. The train station with its overhanging roof. A few
freight cars on side rails, waiting or forgotten. Anders Market
with its wood-planked floor, a great circle of yellow cheese on
a stool inside the front door, the tall shelves lined with clean
white stiff paper. The coffee grinder and scales. The Hatfield
National Bank with its seven barred windows. In Geo. S. Snyder Estate, in the hardware section, the lightbulbs that the
salesclerk tested for you before you paid for them. And out on
the sidewalk people watching Hatfield's first television set in

the tall front window. The great pretzels in Zepp's Bakery and the chest of ice-cold soda in Nick Gerhart's Mobil station. At Pete Wyer's barbershop, men filed in the front door as if to have their hair cut, then out the back door to the taproom of the Knipe Hotel. At I. C. Detweiler's General Store, racks of Clark's thread in all colors. The huge water tower on steel legs at the north end of town. Maybe this portrait inside her head is enough to make the darkness tolerable. This small town which was once freshly painted, everything restored and newly provisioned for the returning soldiers, will be there for her as well when she returns.

Did anyone warn her that one day when she returns from this blackness which people have begun to call her moodiness, and she walks down Market Street to the corner where she can see the school and the church and the train station, suddenly none of it will feel real, none of it will be hers? And she will be left waiting for her own life to begin and suspecting that she does not possess something essential that is required of everyone to live in this place. She will wonder if the normal life will ask a price of her which she cannot meet. The price paid by a neighborhood girl. Maybe the great illusion of life is that we are moving ahead, when, actually, we are always returning, stepping off the train, back again. Or perhaps it is only her; she is the only one who moves against life's momentum.

She draws some consolation from the possibility that these thoughts she has, these dark thoughts, mean nothing at all, nothing profound. They are just the restless thoughts of a teenaged girl with hormones racing through her veins.

But this is a cold consolation and it vanishes completely when she overhears her uncle talking about her father's dark moods. At Lauchman's print shop, where he runs a Linotype press in a room with a dozen other men, her father sometimes goes for a week at a time speaking with none of them. On the hot summer days when they eat their lunches out on the loading dock, he will eat with his back turned to his confederates. Oh, there are other times when he is the life of the party and the center of attention, but he can change his mood without provocation.

She is too much like you, and you're too much like her, she hears her mother telling her father one morning. She is waiting for him to give her a ride to work. It is raining hard, a morning thunderstorm with great sheets of blown rain. She runs through the rain and takes a place in the back seat of her father's car. She will spite him by making him drive her like a chauffeur.

They ride along without speaking a word to one another. The rain is hitting the roof of the car with the sound of buttons poured from a jar. She looks at the back of his head where the hair has begun to turn gray. He has the same naturally wavy hair that she has. They are both the same height now. She is staring at his hand on the steering wheel when suddenly through the rain-streaked passenger window on her right she sees something straight out of a nightmare, an enormous shape rising out of the storm like a great passenger ship and coming right at them. She screams hard and this is enough to rouse her father. He stomps on the brakes, rising up in the seat as he drives the pedal to the floor.

After the train has passed, he drives ahead a little ways then pulls over to the side of the road. His head is bowed and he is breathing hard. You saved our lives, he says to her through his tears. Though she might have wanted to say something to him, or to reach out and touch his shoulder, she keeps her distance and her silence.

Chapter Sixteen

In Grace Lutheran Church the minister, Reverend Fluck, is talking again about the communists who are going to try to take over America. There was something in the news just the other week. A man named Walter P. Reuther, president of CIO United Auto Workers, was shot through the kitchen window of his home in Detroit and everyone knows that communists shot him. Before too much longer they are going to assassinate every public official who refuses to go along with their plans to dismantle everything this great nation holds most dear. Especially the right to worship God and Jesus Christ, the son of God.

Lifting her eyes, Peggy can see the heads nodding in agreement with the minister. Not just the old white heads and bald heads in the congregation, but many heads that are not much older than hers. Her father's head is nodding but her mother is staring out the windows of the church. Jack is leaning against her, placated by a pack of Life Savers, as she gazes serenely out the windows at an empty blue sky. She looks like she is at peace with the world, unthreatened by the communists, or anyone else. The minister's warnings are falling on deaf ears; communists, war, the Russians digging entrenchments in Korea, the man on Cow Path Road digging a bomb shelter in his backyard. All of this is beyond her immediate concern; she is a mother with children to take care of. And once you are a mother in this world, it is something that can never be taken from you. No one can take this from you, and it can surround you and separate you from the rest of the world, enclosing you within an order and a shape so completely defined by its necessity that the great troubles of the world will not matter anymore.

After church she asks her mother what she was thinking about. The farm, she tells Peggy. The farm in Souderton where she grew up.

They have driven by only a few times since the family lost it during the Depression, but her mother has spoken of it often.

An hour later Peggy has made up her mind and arranged everything. She makes a picnic lunch, asks her uncle Howard to drive them there, and then walks her brother, Jack, across town, to leave him with the mother of one of his friends. It is another sunny day, the summer has been a succession of bright days. There is a gentle breeze.

Peggy sits in the back seat with the picnic basket so her mother can ride in front with Howard. He is wearing one of those ditchdigger T-shirts, white with straps over his shoulders. He is tanned and strong, her father's brother, but different from him in small important ways. Howard is carefree, always down on the floor roughhousing with his three little boys. Always putting his arms around his wife, Muriel. She is just a few years ahead of Peggy, still a girl herself, and a source of information about the important things in life that must be explained by someone. What is it like to be in love with a boy? Muriel had responded frankly: When he's away, when he's not in bed with you, you ache for him, I mean you feel this physical pain right through your bones.

Howard drives with the window down, one arm hanging out, his hand cupping his cigarette against the rushing wind. The hard muscles in his tanned shoulders rippled.

At the farm Howard pulls to the side of the road and stops.

What are you stopping for? Peggy's mother asks.

Howard replies with a big grin. I was in the service long enough to learn to do what I'm told to do.

Peggy tells him, Go on up the driveway.

Yes, sir, Howard says, saluting her.

Oh, we mustn't do that, Peg. Her mother worries.

It takes a while for Peggy to coax her mother out of the car.

This is the bank's property, Peg.

Big deal, Mom. Who cares about some stupid bank! The bank didn't live in these rooms—you did.

Peggy is walking ahead when they cross the wide front lawn. The wind is to their backs. When Peggy looks back at Howard he has taken off his T-shirt, lit a cigarette, and is lying across the hood of the car like he owns the place. Peggy laughs and tells her mother to look at him. A smile comes to her mother's face and it is so full of surprise that for a brief moment Peggy glimpses her mother as a younger woman, a girl really. It is such a pleasure to see, such a rare and precious thing. This woman, her mother, if only Peggy could have known her when she was a girl. How unfair that she couldn't have been a friend to her in her youth.

Now, with every step her mother is afraid that someone will come by and see them trespassing. Peggy takes her hand and tells her to stop worrying. It is such a splendid day, such a beautiful moment when the two of them stand before the wood-frame house. The place seems to be waiting attentively for them to climb up the front stairs onto the porch. The windows are not just full of light, but of music, some song that seems to convey itself in her mother's voice.

Their faces are pressed against a window. This is where her grandmother Swan used to do her quilting. And here is where their old dog used to take his naps.

A secret part of her mother is being restored; Peggy doesn't understand it completely, doesn't grasp its whole meaning. At age eighteen she is too young to comprehend fully what the experience of this day means to her mother, how it will manifest itself in her own future. But for now she is trying to delight in her mother's pleasure as she inspects the house through every window.

The kitchen! Oh the marvelous bright kitchen with windows along the front and back walls so you can see straight through the house here. The porcelain cookstove that took either coal or wood. The cabinets with their glass doors. Here is where they spent most of the summer canning food, she tells Peggy. There was a big table right there. Someone has taken the table, but I remember. We would pickle red beets and can them. We put newspapers on the table so we wouldn't stain the wood. When we went to church my mother would make us wear white gloves to hide the stains on our hands.

A picture for Peggy. An image of herself in a sundress, sitting at a table with children of her own, their palms stained red.

They eat the picnic lunch behind a tiny outbuilding which was once an ice shed, in a meadow of juniper and Indian paintbrush. Howard can dispose of a sandwich with three bites. Then he lights a cigarette, lies back in the wildflowers, and blows smoke rings that float above their heads.

You have to eat more than that, Peggy, her mother tells her.

She is eating only carrot sticks and she tries to change the subject. Lately what she eats has become an issue. She has begun to feel that her mother and father, and even her grandmother and grandfather, are trying to fatten her up for somebody's Thanksgiving table. She thinks, *What business is it of yours? It's my stomach! Why don't you leave me alone!*

She has been around long enough to know how the world works, how a girl who grows up to be heavy will hear the same sound over and over in her life, the sound of doors closing just ahead of her. If she's beautiful enough, she can do anything. Maybe she can marry a banker rich enough to buy back her mother's farm!

And one thing she has learned just recently about her beauty is that it is vulnerable. She has lovely hair and fine features in her face, and piercing green eyes, but she can gain weight easily in her legs. She has to be careful. And it doesn't seem fair either. Men are lucky; her father is losing his hair so he has started slicking it down and combing it straight back and he looks as handsome as a politician or a dean. A man gets a fat belly and he just loosens his belt a few notches and takes on the posture of a Supreme Court judge. So easy for men. Not for a girl.

Her beauty is important to her. A validation. Something she can hold between herself and the world, something that lets her off the hook.

It's a man's world, her aunt Sue has told her. Don't let anyone tell you otherwise. And in this world few things count more than beauty does. It can save a farm. Or carry you to Venice to stand at the grave of John Keats.

There is a tire swing hanging from the branch of an apple tree. It takes a long time for Peggy to persuade her mother to sit on it. Kick your legs, Mom, you remember how to swing. Soon she has her mother sailing through the air. Each time she flies forward her dress blows back in the wind and she has to tug it down between her knees. Finally she takes the rope in both hands and her dress flies up around her face. Howard turns to face the road—I didn't see anything! he calls to them.

Chapter Seventeen

Cherry Cokes at Inky's with Adelle who has come home from Ursinus College for the weekend. Her first semester, her first time home as a college coed. Peggy wants to know everything. Adelle can't tell her fast enough. Life in the dormitory. Football games. The professors. The boys. Tearing through town in the rumble seat of some boy's roadster. I always get stuck in the rumble seat, Adelle complains. She is the brainy one, valedictorian in their high school class. Oh, Peg, the best part by far is this feeling that comes over me sometimes when I'm walking across campus. It's like I suddenly remember that I'm on my own, you know? I'm on my own and whatever I do from now on, whatever I make of my life, it's up to me to decide.

She tells Peggy that she simply must come up some weekend and visit her there. The college is only thirteen miles from Hatfield, but it might as well be a million.

You'd absolutely love it there, Peg.

I would? Why?

Oh, you're so pretty, you'd be the center of attention. You're much prettier than the homecoming queen.

Adelle has to explain to her what a homecoming queen is, and the whole time Adelle is telling her, she isn't really listening. She has begun to drift away again on her thoughts. Why hadn't somebody *told her* about college? Whose idea was it that she should spend most of her time in high school taking home economics courses? Learning to sew and cook. What is *home economics* anyway when you compare it to these things Adelle is telling her about?

Take mathematics, for example, Adelle is saying. My professor is an absolute genius. He's teaching us about whole-number theory, Peg. It's brilliant stuff, I'll show it to you sometime.

What is whole-number theory, anyway? Peg asks her.

You remember, we had it in eleventh grade.

Not me. I wasn't in your math class. I took business math. Balancing a checkbook, keeping a monthly budget.

Well, anyway.

Any idiot can balance a checkbook.

I wouldn't say that exactly.

Why not? It's true. I want you to teach me about whole numbers.

They're not really that important.

Yes they are. I want you to teach me about them.

You do?

Yes, right now. Show me right now, Adelle.

On a paper napkin she puts down these numbers: 6, 28, 496, 8,128. These are the perfect numbers, Peg. Each one of them is the sum of a series of consecutive counting numbers. Take 6 for example. 6 equals 1 plus 2 plus 3. And 28 equals 1 plus 2 plus 3 plus 4 plus 5 plus 6 plus 7.

Peg wants to know what the next perfect number is after 8,128?

Yes, tell me.

33,550,336!

Did your professor figure that out?

Oh no, Peg. Everybody's known that for centuries.

Not me. I didn't know it until you just told me.

Adelle goes on explaining how Pythagoras used to play around with the idea of perfect numbers. And Saint Augustine in *The City of God* argues that God took six days to create the world in order to show the world's perfect order. God could have done it in four days or in ten, but he chose six. You see, Peg, mathematics is the language of nature.

What her friend knows is staggering to Peggy. It's enough to take her breath away. Hey, she says to Adelle. Do you want me to tell you how long you bake chicken in an oven set at 325 degrees?

This is part of what troubles Peggy, this feeling of not being smart enough for the world, and once the feeling takes hold of her she begins to hate herself and to slide down the smooth cold wall of the vault again. It is Saturday morning; there is all that time to fill before Monday when she returns to work. Weekends are awful, the way they drag on.

And it gets worse when she is riding in the back of her father's car later in the day. She is looking at her mother in the front seat and her father behind the steering wheel. When they pass the Atlantic station Walter Snyder is out in front in his pale blue coveralls, wiping grease off his hands with a white handkerchief. Walter is Frances Snyder's father. Frances was Peggy's classmate at school until she contracted polio. She was away in Philadelphia for months, lying in an iron-lung machine. Now she is home, living with her father and mother.

Peggy has heard people say that Frances will have to live her whole life with her father and mother.

As they drive along she catches herself tapping the floor of the car each time they pass another telephone pole. She is doing this loud enough for her father to look back at her in the rearview mirror. She can feel the heat rising up her arms, her pulse quickening.

She skips dinner and walks down Main Street to Lincoln Avenue. Leaves are rattling in the cold breeze. Cold? Yes, the first real touch of autumn in the air tonight. Somehow she has failed to notice up until now that the seasons are changing. Too self-absorbed. Too aloof, as they are always telling her.

There is something else she didn't notice; one of her friends has asked her why she stopped singing. She always used to sing when she walked along, but not anymore. Her friend remembers distinctly the time she and Peggy walked up and down Main Street singing that lovely war song—*I'll be seeing you in all the old familiar places* . . . Singing to herself at first and then gradually daring herself to sing a little louder, and then louder still until she wasn't just singing to herself anymore. People were turning on the sidewalk to watch her. It was like she was a character in a musical, the whole town nothing more than a stage set that would be knocked down and carted off at the end of the show.

I'll be seeing you in every lovely summer's day . . .

Those lovely sad lyrics. It is her one true talent, that she can memorize the lyrics to songs on the first time through. Her friends Peg Kirsch and Julia Liedy used to be astonished by this. But it came easily to her. The words entered her. *Used* to enter her.

She is half a block away from where Frances lives on Cherry Street when she sees the green Chevrolet convertible parked at the curb in front of her house. The car owned by the skinny boy who she danced one dance with at Sunny-brook last spring.

She stops on the sidewalk. On the porch of Frances's house she can see this boy leaning against the scrolled railing, smoking and looking out into the street. Like a boy coming to pick Frances up for a date. Frances with her sparkling eyes who will spend the rest of her life in a wheelchair. Frances who will never dance again at Sunnybrook. Frances whose life she will leave behind. For Peggy it is another one of those pictures that will stay in her soul.

A moment later, Frances's father, Walter, wheels his daughter out the front door. The boy turns to greet her. Then he and Walter lift her from the chair. They stand Frances up on her braces. A broken doll in the pale gray light of dusk. From where Peggy stands she can hear the sound of the metal braces clinking. And the steel hinges.

Peggy has come here before when she was feeling sorry for herself, just to remind herself how lucky she is, how purely fortunate she is. Sometimes this works, sometimes the thought of Frances in her iron braces for the rest of her life is enough to shake Peggy from her dark thoughts about herself. Tonight it makes her hope that she will make a better woman than she has made a girl. She hasn't taken orders very well. She has always been in too much of a hurry. And she has never felt connected to this world. Always strangely drifting above it. Not a part of life the way these three people on the porch of the little white house are.

Frances will never walk again. This is what Julia has told her. She will never dance or run to catch the train or make love or have a baby. All of that has been taken from her by polio. The skinny boy and her father are lifting her and moving her forward an inch or two at a time. The sight

of them is enough to make a teenaged girl like Peggy wonder if we have life all wrong. The way we are expected to live
life. We pop out of somebody's belly and then people start
telling us how to live. But what if the people who tell us are
wrong and have always been wrong. All the rules and everything that is expected of us—what if it was all just dreamed
up out of fear? School. Church. Jobs. Marriage. A little
house along a row of houses. All of this was designed to
make us forget that we're all just hanging on to this life by a
thread. All of us like Frances, vulnerable to a sudden turn in
the wind.

When the porch light goes on they are bathed in a light so
bright and clear that Peggy can recognize the boy as the same
skinny boy who danced one dance with her and showed her
his new green convertible the spring before. The boy who
told her about going up and down every street of his hometown after he returned from the army in order to see how he
had changed. That night he was just another soldier back
from the war and eager to grab a dance with any pretty girl
who said yes. There was something he wanted from her and
so her first impression of him was not to be relied upon. But
tonight is different. Tonight she is seeing him as he really is as
he walks the broken girl across her front porch.

A strange feeling comes over Peggy. She will tell only her
closest friend how, as she stood down the street watching him
lift Frances from one step to the next and listening to the
metal leg braces scrape along the porch, she could feel her
hand in his.

At home her father is standing at the kitchen counter
polishing his work shoes. For some reason she tells him, I was
out walking and I saw Frances on her porch with her father
and a young man who was helping walk her.

He tells her that Stan Musial is going to be named Most Valuable Player in the National League for the second straight year.

Men always have their sports to talk about.

He seems to be about my age, she goes on. But I don't remember him from high school.

Her father is spit-shining the black toes of his shoes but he replies that the boy is probably Frances's cousin. I work with her cousin at the shop, he tells her.

What's his name?

Dick Snyder.

It's a name she has heard before, on that night during the war when she and Peggy Kirsch slept outside and rode on the back of Mr. Pugles's vegetable truck with Lorraine who told them about Dick Snyder and his wonderful letters to her after each date.

The same boy Peggy danced one dance with. She has these small pieces of him. He doesn't know that she is alive but she has gathered these pieces of him.

She thanks her father.

What did I do?

For the first time in a long time, she kisses him on his cheek then dances out of the room as he calls to her: *Hey, Peg, what did I do to deserve that?*

Chapter Eighteen

A Saturday morning in December of 1948. Peggy is baby-sitting her ten-year-old brother, Jack, and Muriel's boys. She is walking them down Main Street to watch men climbing ladders and hanging Christmas lights across the town center. She has been sewing navy blue cloth coats for the boys for Christmas and as they run out ahead of her, it is easy to picture them dressed for church in the coats and matching kneesocks.

Little Donnie is four years old. She has to watch him like a hawk. She turns her head for one second and he pulls free of her hand and disappears down the alley behind the barber. When she finds him he has claimed a huge cardboard box as large as a refrigerator that was flattened and left for trash pickup.

She carries the box home and turns it into an airplane for them. With a piece of coal she draws on windows and the machine guns that Jack insists on.

For hours they are in and out of the box, flying missions over Germany while she watches from a porch chair that she has pulled into the sun. Sun finally, after so much rain. So far this winter all the snowstorms have turned to rain. Pennsylvania has had the worst flooding in over a dozen years. The gloom of the weather has settled over everything. Each morning when she awakens to rain, she has to fight the desire to pull the covers over her head, call in sick at work.

It is part of a darkness that seems to be gathering at the far edge of her consciousness. Even today in the sunlight, with the boys' happy voices rising into a blue sky, the darkness is drawing on her. Maybe it is the conversation that she overheard last night. She was at the sewing machine in the kitchen and she could hear her father and Howard talking. Her father had read some crazy spy story in the newspaper. Top secret documents from the State, War, and Navy departments were found on strips of microfilm in a hollow pumpkin on a Maryland farm, and in Washington, D.C., the House Un-American Activities Committee claimed this was definite proof of one of the most extensive espionage rings in the history of America.

The boys want wings for their airplane. They are not satisfied until she has punched holes in two sides of the box and stuck brooms through the holes by their handles.

She sits down again and closes her eyes. Maybe it is all the talk of communists. In Berlin communists have divided the city. American airmen are flying mercy missions across the skies above the city, dropping food and coal for the citizens, to help them survive the winter.

Even on this bright, sunny day with the children's laughter surrounding her, she can feel the darkness running toward her. And a little later when she hears Jack yelling that he is a paratrooper, the cold, smooth walls of the vault close in on her with the vision of the paratroopers caught in trees and on church steeples in the coastal villages of France during the invasion four years ago. She remembers hearing stories on the radio about the German soldiers carefully and slowly taking aim at the paratroopers' heads and shooting them dead where they hung.

The darkness gathering in her soul is matched by some larger darkness in the wider world, and the distance separating the two is shrinking. All the joy of Christmas right after the war is already too distant to recall clearly. Or maybe it is only her? Maybe she is imagining this? Watching the boys lost in their make-believe world fills her with longing for her own childhood.

To try and shake herself out of this mood she joins the boys. She tells her brother, Jack, and his little cousins about the American pilot that the newspapers have called the Candy Bomber. He is flying over Berlin dropping sweets for the children.

Let's pretend we're dropping candy! Peggy exclaims.

But this idea doesn't amuse Jack. He wants to drop bombs.

Bombs AWAY, Peggy! BOMBS AWAY!

One long war over, and another about to begin. Maybe this is the meaning of the cold walls that enclose her.

Finally she leaves them and walks off. For a moment she stands on the cement walkway with her back turned to the boys. She shouldn't leave the boys alone in the yard but a heaviness fills her arms and legs and seizes her with an overpowering need to lie down.

The house is dark and she can hear the rain again when she awakens. Her father and Muriel are standing inside her bedroom doorway. Muriel is saying that everything is fine—so what if the boys ran off to the lumberyard, the worst they could have done was burn the place down, Dave.

Muriel calls goodbye to her, then her father sits on the end of the bed. He bows his head as if he is praying. She wants to return to him, she wants to come back from where her mind has taken her. She tries to make her mind return to the real world by painting a picture again of the town of Hatfield. The loading platform behind the lumberyard. The train station with its overhanging roof. A few freight cars on side rails, waiting or forgotten. The grocery store with its wood-planked floor, a great circle of yellow cheese on a stool inside the front door, the tall crammed shelves lined with clean white stiff paper. The coffee grinder and scales. The bank with its seven barred windows.

And on and on.

It is much later. After midnight. Her mother is waking her to say that something has happened to her father. The ambulance has taken him to the hospital in Sellersville and she is going now to be with him. Peggy will stay at home with Jack who is sleeping.

When she has finished praying for her father she straightens his shoes in the closet, then folds her mother's nightgown and places it beneath the pillow. Then she makes the bed. She doesn't leave the room until she has smoothed out every wrinkle on the bedspread.

She cleans the rest of the house as well. Sweeping the stairs, dusting and scrubbing the bathroom and kitchen floors. She has just finished when Howard comes by to tell her that it was an appendix and that everything is fine.

So she wakes her brother and they ride to Sellersville with Howard. She has been here twice to visit her friend Peg Kirsch who lives in the Nurses' Home which stands just a little ways from the hospital. She has been terribly homesick since she began nursing school. When she calls home she is always crying to her father to please come take her back home. But her mother has insisted that she stay until she finishes school, and she has told Peggy, If my daughter calls you, you tell her from me that if she leaves school, I will personally kick her backside all the way back to the hospital!

Peggy climbs the stairs to the second floor. Her father is in a semiprivate room. Dr. Paul Moyer is sitting on the bed, smoking a cigarette and holding a glass ashtray on his thigh. She leans over and kisses her father's forehead. I want you to meet someone, he says.

The skinny boy steps forward.

Dick, this is Peggy, her father says.

He is holding a hat between his hands. He nods his head and smiles at her. Your father just showed me your picture the other day at work, he says.

I told him that you like to dance, her father says.

Showed him my picture! She is horrified.

Now Dr. Paul joins in. Her father and I delivered her together, how many years ago, Dave?

Seventeen.

Through this, Dick has kept his lit-up smile, nodding his head and turning his hat between his hands. Finally she smiles back at him. From that one dance at Sunnybrook and then when she saw him on Frances's porch, she remembers him as being taller than he really is. If they ever do go out on a date she won't wear high heels.

Chapter Nineteen

They were going to see *Mrs. Miniver*, which is playing at the Strand in Lansdale, but when Dick arrives to pick her up she has changed her mind about that. She prefers to keep things on strictly a "get acquainted" basis. No formal date with this boy who stands next to a printing press beside her father five days a week.

He pulls his car up to the curb and comes bounding up the cement walkway, whistling the song "Peg o' My Heart."

I really don't feel up to a movie and a late night, she tells him at the door.

He doesn't lose his smile. That's fine, he says. He looks into the empty living room. Where is everybody? I thought I'd say hello to your father.

Everybody's next door. My grandparents and my aunt live next door.

That makes it nice, I bet.

My father's afraid I might live at home forever, you see. So whenever I have a date they get out of the way.

A girl like you living at home forever? Not a chance.

Suddenly it begins to rain. When he turns away to the sound of the rain hitting the canvas roof of his convertible she looks him over carefully. His brown wingtip shoes are shined. His flannel trousers are baggy at the knees. He is hipless and his shoulders disappear beneath his tan cable sweater. With his gold-rimmed glasses and his neatly parted brown hair, he looks more like a college student than a printer.

Well, do you want to take a drive, Peggy? he asks her.

A dash through the rain to his car. It's an enormous car. Like stepping into a living room. Or onto an ocean liner. When he starts the engine, she teases him and asks if he wants her to pull up the anchor.

She likes the sound of his laughter.

They have barely driven a block when the rain comes down harder and the roof begins to leak. If you'd put your hand right there, he says. And your other hand over there.

She presses her palms against the ceiling and the rain runs down her arms.

He's sorry, he tells her. The person who owned the car before him didn't care for the roof properly.

It's a fine car except for the roof, he says hopefully. And whenever the sun's out I just put the roof down anyway.

Who needs a roof? she tells him. She is leaning toward him now to keep the rain from dripping down the back of her neck.

Don't you love the rain? he says. When we were going across the Pacific on the army transport ship it was so hot. We were packed in like sardines and it was so hot you could barely stand it. Whenever a shower would pass over, I'd go up onto the deck, lean my head back and just hold my face up into the rain. Before then I never really thought about rain one way or another.

She sees at once that this is a boy who loves to talk. He talks so much, and so well, that she doesn't have to say anything; he fills the silent spaces for her.

They drive past the train station and the Grace Lutheran

Church. At the red light on Main Street it is raining so hard inside the car that he pulls over and parks and they start walking. He wants to show her the house where his grandmother lives. His grandmother is his favorite person in the world.

It is the Amandus Bergey property. Peggy has been by the house a thousand times. Now they stand on the sidewalk in the rain. There are a few lights on in the house. He tells her that his grandmother lives here. Maybe you have heard of her? She's a midwife who delivers babies all over the county. She delivered me and my twin brother in this house.

You're a twin?

Yes.

Your brother, does he look like you?

He tells Peggy that his brother Robert died. At fourteen months, he contracted pneumonia and died.

I had an older brother, Earl, who died too. It's a long story, he says.

Tell me, she says to him.

It's a long story and he tells it without stopping. His mother was raised in an orphanage with her sister. It was a mean place and they were mistreated. One day someone came and took her sister, just like that. His mother wasn't told who had adopted her sister, only that it was a family in Harrisburg. A year went by and then his mother jumped the orphanage wall and ran away for good. She married a man that same year. She was sixteen years old and made the man promise her that if they ever owned a car, he would drive her to Harrisburg so she could search for her sister.

I was four or five and my brother Earl was ten, I think; so ten more years went by before my mother got the chance to go to Harrisburg. It was a long, long trip from Philadelphia in those days. A whole day of driving. I rode in the back seat with Earl. I remember my mother telling the two of us that we were going to find her sister, an aunt we never knew we had. Dad thought it was a dumb idea, but my mother was determined to go.

On the way Earl got a high fever. My mother got in the back seat and held him for most of the trip. When we got to Harrisburg, my father stopped the car on some road and said, "Well, where do you want to go now, Ada?" She had him drive from one neighborhood to another. He drove slowly up and down the streets while she went from door to door.

I watched her, he told Peggy that night of their first date. The front door of each house would open and the people would shake their heads, no. We just kept driving up and down streets and she kept going from door to door, and then she knocked on one door and I saw her fall into someone's arms. Just like that. She had found her sister.

His brother got worse on the way home. Three days later he went into a coma and died.

This story, to Peggy, is the most beautiful and sad story that she has ever heard. Part of it is the music in his voice when he talks, and part of it is the thought that his mother lost a son and found a sister in three days' time.

She looks at his face and she can almost see him as a small boy in the back seat of his father's car, watching his mother go from door to door in a faraway city until she found her lost sister's embrace.

Anyway, he says, I was born in this house. My grandmother delivered hundreds of babies but I was born in a veil and she didn't know what to do. It's like this bubble all around the baby. She had someone call the doctor and he told her just to pop it open.

I've never heard of such a thing, Peggy tells him.

Oh, it's true. It's called a veil. It's supposed to mean that God has chosen you for a special life. It used to be that people would save the veil and sell pieces of it to sailors because even a small piece of a veil was supposed to always keep you safe at sea.

They walk on a ways while he explains to her his grandmother's theory about new mothers. After she delivers a baby she stays with the new mother for ten days. Exactly ten days. One day less and the mother is likely to have problems down the road. But after the tenth day, the new mother is on her own.

What kinds of problems? Peggy asks him.

He doesn't have a clue. I'm just telling you what my grandmother told me, he says, and she laughs to herself about this.

A few days later a letter arrives from him. It is on the kitchen table when Peggy comes home from work. Of course, the boy who wrote letters to Lorraine Pugles after each date! How could she have forgotten?

She opens his letter standing at the sink, her coat still on. It is to thank her for taking the walk in the rain with him. He apologizes if he talked too much and he tells her that she was a very good listener. A good listener like you is hard to find, he has written. This brings a smile to her face. She is still smiling when her mother comes through the front door, calling her name.

She wants to show her something. Follow me, she says.

They walk down Market Street, across Main, to School Street. The first stars are bright in the sky. Peggy has Dick Snyder's letter in her coat pocket. She is playing a game with it, running her fingertips across it, then taking her hand out of her pocket and counting to ten below her breath, then putting her hand back in her pocket to see if it is still there. This makes the letter real. It makes *him* real. She pictures him walking to a mailbox, whistling. Or perhaps driving in his gigantic car with the letter beside him on the front seat. In the two days since the two of them walked through the rain his story has not left her. All day today at work she was trying to think of the precise moments of his life, as if to make his life her own. How they had no plumbing in the house they rented in Skippack when he was a boy and his little sister used to awaken him in the night to take her to the outhouse. She would stand at the door and wouldn't go inside until he had taken the broken handle from an old broom and rattled it around the rim of the seat to clear away the spiders. Then he would remind her to lift up the hem of her nightgown so it wouldn't get dirty.

Peggy fingers the letter in her pocket as she walks down School Street with her mother. She can hear his voice in the rain telling her the story of his mother climbing over the orphanage wall when she was sixteen. And the story of his mother losing her first-born son to pneumonia when he was a boy. How his body lay in his coffin in the living room for two days and how the sound of his mother's weeping filled the house. Her lost boy. Dick was determined to ease his mother's sorrow, so he made a scrapbook of his older brother. On one page he pasted the laces from his brother's last pair of shoes. On another a poem he wrote about the times he and this lost brother used to go sledding down Grumbach's Hill, flying all the way down and hitting the frozen creek at the bottom and gliding across it with their eyes closed so it seemed like they were flying. Sometimes in her sorrow his mother would cry out in her sleep. He would go to her and she would be embarrassed. She would apologize and he would return to his bed and try to keep awake until he was sure she had fallen back to sleep.

He told his stories with a childlike innocence that made them irresistible. This was his gift to her, stories so full of hope that they could enter her. This young man, born in a veil in his grandmother's bed, the only survivor of his mother's three sons, believed his life was intended for something exceptional. He had already told her that God had some purpose for him.

Peggy and her mother have stopped a little ways down School Street. Right here, her mother tells her. What do you think, Peggy?

She tells her that her father has decided to buy this piece of land and to build a new house here. Two hundred and twenty dollars for the land; two more paychecks and the land will be theirs.

Peggy wants to know why they have decided to build a new house now. I won't be living at home too much longer, Mom. You'll have a lot more room once I'm gone.

Her mother smiles and takes her hand. Not this spring, but the following spring is when they will start building the house, but she has already decided on the layout of the rooms. Here is where I'll have my dining room, Peg. You know how I've always wanted a house with a dining room. I'll have windows above the sink so I can see outside while I wash the dishes. The stove here. The refrigerator here.

Peggy helps her mother map out the size of the rooms, one step for each foot.

And a fireplace over here, Peggy. I've always wanted a fireplace in the living room. And bookshelves on both sides, and a big bay window.

She tells Peggy that this will be their dream house. That they will live here the rest of their lives.

Oh, you never know, Peggy says to her. You might end up in Paris, France.

You might, but not me. I'm happy right where I am.

For a moment Peggy watches her mother walking along the borders of this dream house. When Peggy looks up into the sky, there are great mountains of clouds sailing across the face of the moon, clouds that carry her mother's voice away. There are lonely moments between a mother and daughter, moments like this when a daughter can almost picture herself becoming her mother. Despite how different she was determined to make her own life, there is a small house and a plain street waiting for her as well. A moment like this is enough to make a daughter feel the cold, damp earth beneath her feet and a piece of herself drifting toward the heaviness at the center of her body. But what is youth if not a promise? The promise of a letter in Peggy's pocket. She can trace her fingers along the envelope's torn edge and recall the feeling of him standing beside her. It comes on her unexpectedly, the thrill of this; he is standing close enough for her to feel his breath on her cheek, the passing of the words he speaks to her, each word brushing her face. This steadies her, calls her back to her mother in the moonlight, walking the straight lines of her imaginary house.

The sight of her is enough to make a young girl wonder for the first time what a woman's life is in this world. A window where she washes dishes? A place she occupies so often that the world will always see her there even after she has gone? A man can hang his coat up at the end of the day and fall asleep in a chair. He can live his life wherever his shoes are in the morning, without ever revealing himself to anyone, but a woman must open herself to the world in order to be fulfilled. She must find her way past the slamming doors, the rising voices, the walkings out. She must break the silence.

For the last two years Peggy has minded the passing of her mother's youth. Her graying hair. The wrinkles set around her eyes. The little pocket of flesh appearing beneath her chin. A line across your forehead for each child, her mother has said to Peggy. The worrying. The vulnerability. But tonight, lost in the vision of her new house, passing through the moonlight, she looks beautiful and strong, her shoulders outlined against the blue-black sky. She is giving her daughter a glimpse of how strong a woman must be in this life. How strong to open herself again and again to life's possibilities so that one day she can proclaim to the world, I was a person on this earth who took care of children and a man; I put seeds out in the winter for the cardinals; I made a pirate hat out of aluminum foil for my little boy; I wore a hair net to work in a cafeteria to help buy a piece of land where we could build a house; I always broke the silence and filled it with a new chance.

Tonight it is there in front of Peggy, the fullness of her mother's life.

They are standing in the grass, where the porch will be, when her mother tells her what she has never told her before. She knows the restlessness inside her. She had hoped that the dark moods which came over her would have disappeared by now. I guess I've tried to believe all along that you would grow out of it, Peggy. But—

Peggy stops her to ask her please not to say that she is like her father who has never outgrown his own restlessness.

Her mother says that she is sorry, then goes on to ask her

where she goes when she disappears. When you won't speak to anyone for days at a time, where are you, Peggy? All I want, all a mother ever wants, is for her children to be happy. But where do you go, Peggy? Can you tell me where you go when you get in one of your moods?

Where does my father go? Peggy asks her.

I wish I knew.

Did you ever ask him?

Not in so many words. But I've always been here for him when he returns. I've always been standing here, waiting for both of you.

Peggy nods her head. The night has closed in on her.

Children, her mother tells her, little children are the best thing in life. I can't tell you how I missed dressing you. Some days I would sit in a chair with a picture of you as a toddler and I would pray for the chance to get you back, to have you come right out of that picture for just a little while. I wasn't going to keep you for long, I just wanted to hold you for a little while.

Why are you telling me this, Mom?

Her mother takes Peggy in her arms. Babies are the truly best thing in life, she whispers. I'm going to have a baby, Peg.

That night she held her mother at arm's length, her eyes opened wide with the surprise of this. True? she asked.

Yes. True.

When?

October. Next fall. First the baby, and then we'll build the house the following summer. So will you put off Paris or New York City or wherever it is you might go until after I get used to babies again? I'm going to need your help.

Chapter Twenty

He tells her that he has heard that she can sing.

Who told you that?

Your father. He told everyone at work that you have the best voice in the church choir.

He pulls his car into a parking space on Broad Street just around the corner from the Strand Theater in Lansdale.

I'll throw the anchor out, she says to tease him.

I'm going to ask you to sing something sometime, he says. I'm just warning you.

What about you, do you sing?

Me? Oh, no. I dance but I don't sing.

He walks with such a purposeful stride. She is trying to keep up with him and, at the same time, not step on any of the cracks in the pavement. Not stepping on the cracks is the only way that she can keep herself from disappearing with the picture in her mind of her father advertising her to everyone in the print shop. The thought of this is maddening! But she doesn't want to disappear tonight. Not tonight.

The window of the theater is lit like a makeup mirror, bright bulbs around the border. In the center on a stool is a single red rose in a vase, and above the rose the playbill picturing the movie stars. Greer Garson is a stunning beauty.

Hey, she looks like you, Dick calls to Peggy. He is already at the door, holding it open for her, telling her that it feels cold enough to finally snow. As she steps past him through the door, his hand brushes her back then rests against her waist. This might be nothing more than his good manners. It might not mean anything.

The news comes first. THE MARCH OF TIME . . . Churchill has given a speech in Boston. He says that communists would have overrun Western Europe and attacked Britain within the past three years had they not been afraid of the U.S. atomic bomb.

This dark news. Such a contrast to what she wants to feel. Why must all the joyous moments in her life be set alongside talk of war. Will they ever stop talking of war?

This boy beside her who touched her back just a few minutes before is lost in the gloomy news. The black-and-white images from the screen are reflected in miniature on the lenses of his rimless glasses. This first date will be a bittersweet memory.

There is an orchestra in the theater playing an old song from the war, a song she knows the lyrics to, and she begins saying them to herself below her breath to try to block out the news.

> For all we know, we may never meet again.
> Before you go, make this moment sweet again.
> We won't say goodnight, until the last minute,
> I'll hold out my hand and my heart will be in it.
> For all we know, this may only be a dream.
> Tomorrow may never come for all we know. So love
> me tonight, tomorrow is made for some, tomorrow
> may never come for all we know.

She has known the words to this song for a long time, but before tonight they did not mean what they mean now; with Dick beside her the words tell the sadness of two lovers parting. Love made the war more hateful, more unbearable.

He tells her something he will always remember; he was on a ship heading for the invasion of Japan. A million or more GIs were expected to die in this invasion. Then the bomb was dropped. When he arrived in Japan, everywhere he went the Japanese fell to their knees and begged him not to kill them.

It made me feel guilty, he tells her. And it made me see that life isn't fair, just as people say it isn't. It isn't fair, people say. Well, we're lucky that it isn't. Because if it was fair, then we would have to share the grief of those people. The world's grief would be shared equally.

He has such big ideas. The way his mind works reminds her of her friend Adelle, off at Ursinus College.

You ought to go to college, she tells him.

Oh yes, he says. I'm thinking about it. I've already written to the University of Pittsburgh; they have a mechanical engineering degree. I could go on the GI Bill. I may apply. But first I'm going to learn how to build a house.

Oh?

Your father is going to teach me. I'm going to come over after work once spring is here and the days are longer.

Not this spring, she tells him. Next year he's going to build the house.

Right, next year. Will you still be around then?

Me?

Yes, you.

She smiles when she says this: Oh, you never know, I may be living in Paris by then.

He takes her seriously and asks what she plans on doing there.

Singing, she replies. I'm going to sing in the little cafés, the sidewalk cafés.

That's an excellent plan. I can see you doing that.

You can?

Absolutely. You'd sell a lot of coffee.

Well, it's not really a plan. It's more like a dream.

Dreams are good, he tells her. I think dreams are the most important thing a person can have.

When the movie begins, it looks like a dream itself. The men are handsome and they always know just what to say. The women are beautiful. Even in the morning the wives are dressed like Cinderella. And they live in magnificent white houses that are separated from the sidewalk by picket fences. The people who live in these houses have time to dress for dinner. The houses are all spacious and the little children say the most clever things.

And then the atmosphere of the story changes dramatically. This little town is an English village, and soon Hitler's planes are dropping bombs on the dream. The pretty young bride, played by Teresa Wright, is eighteen years old, Peggy's age exactly. She has just married the young British RAF pilot. There is a scene of them returning by train from their honeymoon, ready to begin their splendid, charmed life together. And then, five minutes later, the bride is dead, shot full of holes by a strafing Nazi airplane.

Who in the world except her aunt Muriel will understand how she feels when her heart sinks into sadness? It's only a movie, she tells herself, it's just a silly movie. It isn't real. Isn't real. But it's as real as anything else and she can feel herself beginning to fall away. This isn't supposed to happen on her first real date with him and she tries to concentrate on something other than the sadness of the story. She tries to think of work tomorrow to distract her. The girls at work will want to know all about her date. Well, it was very nice. The Strand was showing that old war movie, *Mrs. Miniver*, and it was . . . no, it was strange and I cracked up. No. No. Sledding! Yes, sledding. Think about that beautiful picture he painted of how he used to go sledding down the hill in Skippack when he was a boy and if he could turn at the right moment, he could make it onto the frozen creek and glide forever.

She closes her eyes and pictures him as a boy flying on his wooden sled, the speed making wind and the wind making his eyes water. The metal runners catching the hard ice and sending him off down the creek. Her eyes are closed and she is trying hard to stay on the wooden sled with him and to feel the joy of this ride. But the ice is cracking all around her, pulling free from the banks of the creek, opening up great holes in front of her. And somehow she falls off the sled, into one of the holes. Before she goes down below the ice she can see him sailing away from her. He will glide along forever, oblivious to the cold, black water and the raging currents beneath the ice that have caught her.

What breaks this spell is the sound of his voice asking her if she is all right. Are you all right, Peggy?

Before she turns to reassure him that she is fine, she discovers that she has been gripping both arms of the red plush chair. She looks down at her hands. She can't look at him now or he will know.

On the way out of the theater she stops in the rest room

and leans over the sink, splashing cold water on her face. When she raises her head she can't look at her face in the bright mirror.

Outside he is talking a mile a minute about how fantastic the show was and how they must be the only two people on earth who didn't see that movie when it came out in 1942. Well, you were probably too young, he is saying. And I—

She doesn't hear the rest because his voice is drowned out by an airplane groaning in the dark sky overhead.

She is aware that she is hiding some part of herself from him, even now. Maybe she doesn't want to diminish the light of the world that he believes in. That would be unforgivable, wouldn't it? To take this boy with all his joy and optimism and pass on her darkness to him. He believes in his future, he believes that all the bad things are behind him now, finally behind him, the death of two brothers, the war, all of this is behind him and he can hear the music in everything now, he is connected to the goodness of life. The fact that he has survived is reason enough for him to believe in his future.

But the airplane overhead is flying low in the sky and she is lost in the groaning engine and in the memory of her father looking up into the night sky during the war. She can still picture him tipping his head back and looking straight up into the sky. The tiny red and green blinking lights passing across the stars.

Suddenly she asks him if he would have to go if there were another war.

Sure, he says. He's still on active reserve status in the army. He would be the first to go. He wants to tell her a funny story though; his uncle Linford, his father's brother, was excused from the war because he was a conscientious objector. He was an insurance salesman and he called Dick right after Pearl

Harbor and asked him to come talk to him. So he went to see him in his office and his uncle told him that he should think about applying for conscientious objector status himself because if ever there was anybody who wasn't suited to kill another person it was Dick Snyder. But Dick told him that he planned to go in as soon as he finished school. He thanked his uncle for the advice but he had made up his mind to go do his best.

Well then, his uncle said to him, if you're determined to go, I can sell you a fine life insurance policy.

Peggy can hear Dick's laughter. And she is trying to follow the sound of it back to where she is standing by his side. She is looking into his eyes when he tells her that this is why he survived, this is the reason, to be here with her. She can tell that he is never going to judge her harshly. He will never try to make her become something that she doesn't want to be. And when he takes her hand she is aware of her body moving, not spinning or dizzy with anticipation, just moving calmly and thoughtfully. It is a strange, inexplicable feeling that she is returning from a hard and tiresome journey. He is going to help her complete her return. And maybe love is nothing more complicated than turning to look at him and finding that he is already looking at her. He is there waiting for her to return. And then, as easily as if she had looked up into the sky and found the night stars there, his hands are on her shoulders, the tip of his nose brushes across her lips, and then her mouth is beneath his; cool and comforting, as if he is bestowing a prayer upon her, he kisses her. She can hear a sigh escape his lips. How his touch transports her. It carries her away from her father's house, her lined-up shoes in the closet, her clothes folded neatly in tissue paper. This is what she has been searching for her whole life, to be touched like this. It stills some turmoil, just as she has seen the young mothers still their babies' cries. His touch is like a blessing. And to be worthy of it, to earn his touch, she must conceal the darkness inside her, she must never allow her darkness to contaminate the marvelous fine light surrounding him. Though the light does not belong to her, it spills into her path, the path that the two of them are already following, and if she does anything to dull this light or to extinguish it, they will both be lost in the darkness.

And then he thanks her for the kiss.

Write me a letter tomorrow and tell me about it, she says to him.

He will. He says, I think I'll write it and bring it by myself.

She will wait for him to come up the cement path from the sidewalk to her door. She already knows that she doesn't want anyone else to have him. Before she knows what love is, she knows this.

The next time she is alone with her aunt she will tell her about this date. She will try to explain how he was so eager to touch her that she could feel him even before he placed his hand on her. And it was because of this that she fell in love with him, not thinking about marriage and children or any of that—but because of this marvelous thing, the way he touched her before he set his hand on her, this made her decide simply that no other girl should have him. That he should be hers.

BOOK THREE

Chapter Twenty-one

I didn't see it then, but now I see clearly that when we pledge our passions to life we are brought within reach of the mysteries that surround us all, and which circle above time and reason and explain the fierce longings of our souls. I see now that my search for Peggy was the spiritual journey I had begun as a child when the face of my mother was revealed to me on the column of white light that glided across my bedroom. I am not a religious man and never have felt anything more than restlessness in the presence of my father's religion. But that winter I built a small shrine to him and Peggy on the table beside my bed where I placed three photographs of them and the small blue rattle someone had given them when I was born. I included the invitation to the baby shower that Peggy purposely mailed too late for any of her friends to attend, and the only letter I would ever have that she had written to her best friend telling her that she had just learned she was pregnant.

I began waking at four o'clock in the morning to sit before the bedside table as if it were an altar. I would make the sign of the cross on my forehead and then close my eyes and wait for the first sentence of their love story to reach me through the layers of darkness that were the sad reflections of my boyhood. I suppose that I was worshipping my mother for the first time—or worshipping the memories I never had of her—in the still emptiness of these early morning hours, a holy emptiness that was gradually filled by her voice. And her voice, after such a long silence, was more welcome to me than the air I was breathing. The nearest I can come to describing how those early hours felt when I awakened and turned my eyes to the photographs is that I felt like I was falling in love. Each new morning I fell in love again.

One day before dawn I was told that I would find the end of my mother's story in a cold place, far away from where her story was leading me now.

And on another morning, in the predawn darkness it came to me that I should watch the movie *Mrs. Miniver.*

I watched it at night when Colleen and the children were asleep, and when it turned out to be the story of a girl my mother's age who dies suddenly, leaving her grief-stricken husband behind, it sent chills across my skin. When I stood up, I couldn't feel my feet beneath me. I felt like I had been transported back across time and was sitting in the dark theater in Lansdale, Pennsylvania, watching with my father and Peggy as they saw *but could not see* the story of their own lives unfold on the movie screen in front of them. It seemed to me that Fate had arranged the events of their life so that on their first real date they ended up sitting in a movie theater watching an invented story that would soon become the story of their hearts' passage.

I sat staring at the empty television screen long after the movie had ended. I went upstairs from room to room hoping that Colleen or one of my children was awake so I could tell them what I had just seen. But everyone was sleeping contentedly.

I felt very warm, and then very hot, and I went to the front door and opened it and stood in the cold winter air. It was snowing so hard that I couldn't see across the street. I put on my coat and boots and walked down to the beach where a low wind off the ocean was driving the snow. With my head bowed I marched along on sand beneath my feet that was frozen hard like concrete. I knew then that in the mysteries I could not explain, I would find the truth of Peggy's love story. And very soon then the mysteries began to reveal themselves to me.

I am back in the nursing home, visiting my grandfather again. He gives me a handwritten letter that he has found for me. At the top of the letter is the date, August 13, 1977, and then these words written to my grandmother:

> Peggy's death was caused by pregnancy toxemia, cerebral hemorrhage and anemia. The toxemia would be kidney failure, this is why she had so much fluid retention. The cerebral hemorrhage would be like a stroke, either a clot or bleeding in the brain area. The anemia would be not enough red blood cells. I remember that Peggy's hemoglobin was only 47% when she was discharged from the hospital. I would think the main cause of her death was the toxemia, and of course that was greatly due to improper care on her doctor's part.

The letter is signed. And to the right of the signature are the letters *R.N.*

"A nurse," I say to my grandfather.

The room he has transformed into a gallery of his daughter's photographs is cast into deep silence. He looks at me and nods his head slowly.

Nineteen seventy-seven. Twenty-seven years after Peggy's death, a nurse writes a letter to her mother, my grandmother, whom I only knew as a blue-eyed, beautiful woman who scattered seeds across the snow for the cardinals who flew into her yard in the winter.

My grandfather tells me that I can keep the letter as I am reading the last line again . . . "I would think the main cause of her death was the toxemia, and of course that was greatly due to improper care on her doctor's part."

"Why wait all those years to write this letter?" I ask him.

He tells me that my grandmother's heart was failing her in 1977; there was the possibility that she might not live much longer and she was desperate to find a nurse who could tell her if Dr. Wright had been responsible for Peggy's death. He remembers this: "When your mother came home from the hospital with you boys, she got weaker and weaker. Your grandmother called Dr. Wright every day, but he told her there was nothing more he could do for her."

On the way back home from Pennsylvania the next day, I stop in New York City to see the Taft Hotel where Peggy and my father went on their honeymoon. Of course the hotel was knocked down years ago. In the Public Library I read old newspaper accounts of the hotel. By the time Peggy and my father stayed at the Taft, it was already famous in New York as the place where young women went to jump to their death from the rooftop dance club. A month after my mother and father checked out of the hotel at the end of their honeymoon to begin their married life together, a nineteen-year-old girl jumped into a crowd of five thousand spectators who had gathered below on Seventh Avenue.

I read this in the New York Public Library, then drive back to Maine, thinking how close the angel of death was to my mother even then, on her honeymoon.

Chapter Twenty-two

O f all the strange and unlikely possibilities, Dr. Wright is still alive. My daughter Erin looks up at me from the chair where she is reading when I cry out in my astonishment.

"He's still alive!"

A retired nurse has seen him in Lansdale, in a supermarket. She found his telephone number and address, then called my uncle Jack.

I go upstairs to my bedroom and turn on the night-light that illuminates the altar on the table beside my bed. My hands are shaking as I pick up the telephone.

He is eighty-eight years old, he tells me.

"You've lived a long life, doctor," I tell him.

He replies, "I can assure you that on most days I don't consider it a privilege to have lived so long."

I tell him who I am.

"Yes," he says. "I saw the article in the newspaper."

I tell him that I'd like to come see him to talk with him about my mother who was his patient.

He says at once that he doesn't remember a patient by that name and that none of his mothers ever died.

"I delivered over a thousand babies and I never lost a mother," he says.

I remind him that Peggy was only nineteen years old when she died.

"Yes," he says calmly. "I read that in the newspaper."

"We were your first twins," I tell him. "My father remembers you telling him that we were your first twins. You told him you were going to mark the occasion by charging him for only one baby."

"No," he says, "I don't remember any of that. I'm sorry."

He is polite, soft-spoken, sure of himself, so sure of himself that he is completely unsurprised, as if he had been waiting for me to reach him. I am left feeling that he is withholding something from me.

This is the beginning of something I cannot stop even if I wished to. This is where the iron wheel is set rolling on a track that will lead me to the purpose for my life. I am sure of it, and two days later when I am a hundred miles from home, teaching a short story by John Cheever to a class of college freshmen, someone knocks on the classroom door and tells me there is an urgent telephone call from home.

Down the glassy corridor to the telephone, the sunlight reflecting off the snow casts a band of gold ahead of me. I feel weightless, a rush of cold air swirling in my lungs.

It is Colleen. "Something came for you in the mail this morning from the North Penn Hospital."

I remember the woman who sat at her desk in the office of medical records. All the records from the Elm Terrace Hospital had been destroyed, she told me.

She has sent an index card that was taped to the rail of my mother's bed. "Read it to me," I tell my Colleen.

Peggy L. Snyder. Delivery at full term. Diagnosis: preeclampsia. Dr. Edward Wright. The doctor's name was typed just below his signature.

What this means is, forty-seven years after my mother died, I know what killed her. And I know that no matter what he has told me, Dr. Edward Wright was my mother's doctor.

The next week a woman named Joannie Murray called me to say that her cousin sent her the newspaper story about my mother. She told me that in 1954 she almost died of extreme toxemia during a pregnancy. A condition called preeclampsia. In 1954 she was twenty-five years old and had a two-year-old son and a four-year-old daughter. It was summer and she was in the fifth month of her pregnancy when she began to feel as if she was losing her mind. Her face had swollen to nearly twice its normal size. She was suffering excruciating headaches and for hours each day her vision was so blurred that she couldn't see across the room. One day in the middle of making lunch for her children she dropped a can of tomato soup onto the kitchen floor and this angered her so terribly that she began to hit the wall with her hand. She was watching herself hitting the wall and telling herself to stop, but she couldn't. Soon both children were screaming with fear. She hit the wall even harder, trying to drown out their screams. She didn't stop until she had punched a hole in the plaster.

A woman living in the upstairs apartment came to see what the noise was all about, and then called Joannie's physician.

She was hospitalized, first for three days during which time the preeclampsia was diagnosed, and then after another month at home, for six weeks. It was a Catholic hospital.

Joannie was Catholic and so were her husband and her doctor. During her second hospitalization she began to suspect that she wasn't being told everything by the medical staff. She had made friends by then with a red-haired nurse, an Irish girl who eventually confided in her that she was in grave danger. The only cure for preeclampsia was delivery of the baby. If she carried the baby to full term she would most likely die. In fact, she was in great danger if she didn't have the baby delivered prematurely before the seventh month.

Because preeclampsia is a condition where the fetus is poisoning the mother, the only cure is to take the baby. But the Irish nurse told her that the Catholic Church held a clear and unwavering moral position in such cases: the mother was always to be sacrificed in order to allow the baby the greatest possible chance to survive.

In Joannie's case, her husband and physician had agreed to keep from her the full account of her condition. The doctor instructed the nurses on the floor not to tell her that her life was threatened by the baby. They were to keep her as calm and as comfortable as possible.

After the Irish nurse broke the silence, Joannie had her mother arrange for her to be transferred to another hospital where, before she told her husband that she was going to give up the baby, she found a sympathetic doctor who did an emergency cesarean. Her four-months-premature baby boy did not live, but Joannie survived. "I had two children at home who I had to live for," she told me. "At least this is what I have made myself believe all these years."

That night I sat in the kitchen with the index card that had once been taped to the rail of my mother's bed. I wanted to believe that she had touched this card, had brushed her fingers across it.

I brought the card up to my bedroom and placed it on the altar with the photographs and the baby rattle and as I stared at the words—Peggy L. Snyder. Delivery at full term. Diagnosis: preeclampsia. Dr. Edward Wright, and the doctor's signature just above his typed name—I began to wonder if it was possible that my mother had carried my brother and me to full term without the knowledge of what this would do to her. If she had died in the name of some religious code. My grandfather had been a fervent churchman, he had practically started the Lutheran church in Hatfield. Was it possible that Dr. Wright had explained the preeclampsia to him and he had spoken with his minister and they had made a decision without consulting my mother? This might explain my grandfather's tears whenever he spoke about Peggy, and the gallery of photographs he lived with in the nursing home.

I already know that this sort of thing could have happened. After my mother died I went to live with my father's mother—a woman I called Nana, who became the center of my world. She died when I was fourteen of a horrible stomach cancer which filled the little house where she lived on Towamencin Avenue with a smell so rancid that it clawed at my eyeballs. The doctor and my father's father had made the decision that it was better for her if she wasn't told what was wrong with her. They told her she just had the stomach flu. She had to know that people with the flu don't smell the way she smelled. But no one ever told her the truth.

Not even my father, her only son. He must have believed it would be better for her. He must have kept his silence out of love for her.

My father. My mother's husband, a man who believed that God had chosen him for a special purpose. A man who saw the goodness in all things and whose faith in the divine order of things was childlike and unyielding. He believed that Peggy was a gift from God. Could he also have believed then that her life was in God's hands?

What if my father knew? My father who, in his grief over losing Peggy, declared himself to blame for her death. My father who, ten years after her death, decided to go to the seminary to become a minister and devote himself to God. Could this have been an act of penance?

Was it possible that my grandfather and my father had placed my mother in God's hands, telling themselves that because they were doing the right thing by the Church, God would protect her from harm, and them from losing her?

That night I lay in bed listening to the branches of a tree rattle against the window. After a while it began to sound like someone was trying to get in from outside. It went on for hours and then I went out into the backyard and snapped the branch off with both hands. I threw the pieces as far as I could into the dark night.

On the altar was the index card that had changed everything. It was in writing: my mother didn't die because Dr. Wright had failed to make the proper diagnosis of her condition. He had known of her condition from the first time she visited him in January of 1950. He had done the urine test then and found the presence of protein. He had noted her high blood pressure and with these two things in mind he had told her that she would have to have her baby in the Sacred Heart Hospital in Norristown. She then told her husband and her mother and father. They all went to talk with the pastor of the Grace Lutheran Church. The law was laid down, and my mother was sentenced to death.

· · ·

This is a new reason not to sleep at night. I sit in bed staring at Colleen asleep beside me. Should I tell her how little I thought of my dead mother across the years of my life? In 1985 when we were living in Iowa City expecting our first child I thought of Peggy because I thought that I might lose Colleen like my father had lost her. Then another five years passed before I thought of her again. Maybe it had been ten years since I had last thought of her.

Finally I get out of bed and call my brother who is a Lutheran minister. I ask him to find out for me what the Lutheran Church's position would have been in 1950.

"I already know," he says. "I've been thinking the same thing, so I checked. The Lutheran Church held the same position as the Catholic Church."

I feel a slow burning anger rise inside me. I imagine my mother growing sicker and sicker and no one telling her why.

In my nightmare, the same five men are standing at Peggy's grave. The moon is bright and a narrow band of light sweeps over their heads. These are the five men who have outlived her. The doctor who delivered her babies. Her father. Her husband. Her twin sons. They are all standing on the earth in her absence. All of them are gray-haired men now. Compared to her astonishing beauty, what a sorry sight they are there at her grave.

No wonder no one ever took me to this grave or told me anything about my mother's life. No wonder I never asked; a part of me must always have known that I was to blame.

I am thinking this in my half sleep as I watch the five men standing at my mother's grave. None of them boys, none of them young anymore. All of them have outlived her. Her father at ninety. Her doctor at eighty-eight. Her husband at seventy-one. Her twin sons at forty-seven. We have all out-lived her. Conspirators in her death, the death that claimed her at age nineteen. How can we justify our living? How can we ever sleep through the night knowing that we lived on for so long after her life was finished?

I feel blood on my hands. My part in her destruction.

I place another telephone call to Dr. Wright. "Are you sure you can't remember her, sir?"

This time he tells me that he has checked his records and he never had a patient by her name.

Chapter Twenty-three

In the predawn light of those February mornings I felt like I was trying to pick a thread up off the dark floor. I was close to something, I knew that, but it would never stay between my fingertips long enough for me to hold it to the light. At times it felt like it was something I had once possessed, maybe some knowledge that I had always carried with me.

A neighbor of Peggy's who lived three doors down Market Street in 1950 told me that though my mother was living there in her parents' house, she never saw her after April and she didn't think Peggy went outside at all the whole summer until the morning of August 9 when she saw her hobbling barefoot down the cement walkway in the backyard. She was barefoot, her feet were swollen like blocks of wood and her face was twice its normal size. The neighbor watched Peggy slide into the front seat of her father's car and drive away. That was the day she went into Elm Terrace Hospital to be delivered.

I planned another trip to Pennsylvania at the end of the winter. My brother was going to meet me there and we were going to go see Dr. Wright. It was my idea not to tell him that we were coming; I was afraid he would find a reason not to be there. And I wrote him a long letter which I hoped would make it easier for him to open his door when we stood there knocking:

Dear Dr. Wright:

I am writing you now to apologize. For the past fifty years some people in the Snyder and Schwartz families have believed that you were negligent during the time when Peggy was your patient. Stories of your disregard for her have stood as truth and were passed on to me and my twin brother across the years. Peggy's mother, my grandmother, went to her grave believing in her heart that you didn't care for her daughter and that was why she died.

The story that persisted all these years was that you never should have released Peggy from Elm Terrace. And when she was home for seven days someone finally summoned Dr. Paul Moyer, Peggy's family physician, who came over and when he saw Peggy, he remarked with anger, "This is not the Peggy I know." He immediately summoned an ambulance and had Peggy taken to Grandview where she died less than an hour later.

But I have received something in the mail which shows that none of this is true, Dr. Wright. Though all hospital records from Elm Terrace were destroyed when the new hospital was built, I was sent an index card that apparently had marked Peggy's chart while she was in Elm Terrace as your patient in 1950. The card reads: Peggy Snyder. Admitt. Diag. Pregnancy at term. Preeclampsia. Final Diag. Same. Service of Dr. Edward H. Wright.

That one word, Dr. Wright, preeclampsia, is enough to make me see now that those who have blamed you for my mother's death are wrong. That one word has compelled me to see in a different light everything else I have learned about Peggy's life in the last year of my research and writing. It has enabled me to answer so many questions. First, why did Peggy have you instead of Dr. Moyer for her physician; Dr. Moyer had been her doctor since she was a young girl. He had been her mother's physician less than a year before and had delivered her mother's baby in October of 1949.

Why? Because when Dr. Moyer examined Peggy for the first time and discovered that she was pregnant, he also discovered in her urine test that there was protein present, and that her blood pressure was unusually high—both told him that she was probably going to face a difficult pregnancy with pre-eclampsia. So, he referred her to you, a more experienced physician with expertise in obstetrics.

Why did Peggy write to a friend as early as January 1950 that she was going to have her baby in Sacred Heart Hospital in Norristown? Because you advised her that it was a much more sophisticated hospital than Elm Terrace, one where a prematurely delivered baby would have a better chance to survive.

Why does my father remember you telling him not to let Peggy eat any salt?

Because you were right on top of the diagnosis of preeclampsia.

Why did Peggy move back home with her parents in the fourth month of her pregnancy? Because you cautioned her that she was in for a rough time. I believe it is even possible that you told her the only cure for her condition was to have the baby delivered by cesarean, before the seventh month. You told her that if her pregnancy continued any longer than this, her condition could be fatal. But when you told her that the baby might not live if it was delivered early, I believe the Schwartz and the Snyder families, because of their deep religious beliefs, either persuaded Peggy or simply acquiesced to her desire to carry the baby to full term. And if this is true, Dr. Wright, then it explains why the family was never able to face the truth across the years and why you were blamed; anything less would have meant that they were partially responsible for Peggy's death. They had "placed her in God's hands," with their religious belief that the baby was meant to be spared in cases like this. And then when Peggy died, they blamed you.

That is my story, Dr. Wright. The story of Peggy Snyder who died when she was nineteen years old because she carried me and my brother to full term in her pregnancy. I believe that you did everything possible to help her and to save her life but the family's wishes ran against your recommendation that Peggy's baby be delivered prematurely.

Again, my sincere apologies to you for the incorrect assumptions and the falsely held beliefs about you all these years. Someday this spring I will try to come see you with my brother, David, so I can apologize to you in person.

Best regards,

I couldn't be sure of any of this, but I sent the letter anyway and for a little while I pretended to know all the answers and to finally hold the reasons in my hands.

I soon had three wedding photographs to place on the altar beside my bed. Each of them showed Peggy in her wedding dress, and whenever I looked at them they set my heart racing. It had been more than forty years since she visited me in my room, but I remembered that this was the dress that she was wearing when she glided toward me on a column of light, calling me by my first and middle names. White satin. Delicate embroidery across the low neckline. The dress spilling like a pool of milk around her feet.

In the photographs she is holding white satin ribbons at her waist. A flowered headband in her hair holds the white-laced veil.

She only visited me for a brief time in my life. It was 1955. My father had just remarried and the four of us had moved into the little house on Clearspring Road in Lansdale. My brother, Dave, and I shared one of the two bedrooms on the first floor and this is where Peggy visited me. I don't know why Dave never woke up to see her. I would awaken with the knowledge that she was there, waiting for me to open my eyes. It is the way I've often awakened in the night, knowing that it has begun to snow.

I suppose it makes sense that she would have visited when she did; she would have wanted to see what our life was like now that she had been replaced. I imagine she stood over Dick as he slept beside his new wife. She would have seen the lines in his face, how he had aged in the five years since she left him. She would have noticed that he never smiled the way he used to. He never danced like he danced with her.

Long after her last visit to my bedroom, I tried to will her back. One Christmas I asked for an alarm clock. I remember everyone thought this was very strange of me. It was a wind-up clock with a black face and white hands and numerals. I used to set it for two or three o'clock in the morning, and then once it woke me I would make myself stay awake, waiting for her. I didn't even know who she was. It was four years later before my father told us about her. I didn't know who she was but I was waiting for her to take me with her. This I remember distinctly. Wanting to go with her wherever she went when she left me in my room.

Staring at her wedding pictures, I know that there are things about her I will never know. I know that she took more than her share of secrets with her. But I could almost hear her now, I could almost hear her voice telling me not to stop searching for her until I knew fully who she had been in this world when she was here among the people who have all grown so unspeakably old in her long absence.

Chapter Twenty-four

Peggy's mother cooks pot roast every Sunday. Pot roast with potatoes and carrots in the same pan. She has the oven set to cook dinner while they are all in church. Soon Dick is with them every Sunday. In church he sits next to Peggy's mother and father, never taking his eyes off her in the choir. Whenever she glances at him, he is smiling up at her with a richly contented expression. The look of someone who has found what he was searching for.

After the service they all walk back to the house for dinner. He sits at one end of the table, Peggy sits to his right next to her mother. Sometimes her grandfather and grandmother, her aunt Sue, her aunt Anna, and her aunt Lilly join them. It reminds Dick of the Depression years when his mother's and father's brothers and sisters shared a rented house with his family. He recalls them as good years. Hard, but good, because everyone was so close. He remembers his mother trying to make a dinner out of only a half-dozen potatoes. His father coming home at the end of the day with a few nickels, his hands and face dark blue from the cold. But there were those marvelous evenings spent in the crowded living room, singing and listening to the radio. Everyone so close. Everyone in the same boat.

He talks and talks, having second helpings, then thirds.

Where does he *put* all that food! So skinny, so much like a little boy. The story of his life unfolds. When he was in ninth grade his father came home one day with a typewriter. He set it on the kitchen table and said there would never be enough money for college so Dick should learn to type. Here is your future, his father said to him. It will take you to a better life than the one I've had. The typing might have saved his life; in the army he was assigned as a clerk-typist rather than shipped to the Battle of the Bulge. His whole life has been like this, one small miracle after another. In 1941 when shortages of gasoline forced his family to move from Skippack into Lansdale so his father could ride the train to work in Philadelphia rather than use the family car, Dick lived right next door to Jack Graham who would be his friend for life. Jack was the big, affable captain of the Lansdale High School football team. He knew that Dick was far too slight to play football, but he encouraged him to become the team's waterboy and manager and this placed him in the circle of the best group of friends a kid could ever want. There was Jack, Lentz Tiffany and Roy Meyers, Tom Pugles and Bill Crockett.

One Sunday Dick talks about how he was the chaplain's assistant in the army when he was stationed in the Philippines. He enjoyed the work very much and feels that someday he may go on to seminary and become a parish minister. Or perhaps he'll become an engineer or an accountant. Whatever it is, it's only a matter of picking. All the doors are open to him now. America has come into her destiny, everything is under a bright coat of paint, a good life is available to anyone who is willing to work hard. No dream is beyond reach. He believes this. Deeply believes this because his whole life has been a miracle.

Here is a young man for whom everything seems possible. When he is in the house, Peggy is so relieved to be able to just sit here and not have to make conversation. For the first time in her life, she is out of the spotlight of center stage, standing in the wings and watching. He talks and talks, filling her house with such optimism and music that the moment he says goodbye, oxygen begins to drain from the rooms and Peggy follows him out onto the porch, wishing, as he drives away, that she could go along with him. Sometimes she will put on her coat and sit on the top step of the porch to wait for him to return.

And sometimes she will push him away. Why, she doesn't really know. It just comes over her, she wants to incorporate herself in him and run away from him at the same time. Maybe because she doesn't feel that she deserves his goodness. Maybe because she wants to see just how strong his affection for her is. She will push him away to show him how unworthy she is of his love and to see how much he loves her. Pushing him away accomplishes both.

It confuses her. The worst of it happens one night at Sunnybrook when she and Dick are there with all his wonderful friends. Tom Pugles, so handsome that when he goes to the Nurses' Home at Grandview Hospital in Sellersville to pick up his dates, all the student nurses run to the front windows just to get a look at him. And Bill Crockett, who works at Lauchman's print shop with Dick and who calls Peggy "Doll." And Jack Graham, the big football player with his sleepy smile, as friendly as a big teddy bear. And Lentz Tiffany, with baby blue eyes, who can clear off the dance floor with his jitterbug moves. Peggy is watching them, watching Dick surrounded by such marvelous friends. There is something about the way he carries himself in their presence; he doesn't compete with them, he observes them, as if he were the one in the group whose responsibility it is to remember these fine times that they are sharing. He is grateful for each of them. He seems so thankful that they have chosen him to be in their company. This is Dick Snyder and she is thankful for him. But still she excuses herself from the table and walks away. She finds a place where she can sit and watch them without them seeing her. She sees Dick get up from the table to go looking for her. Twice he leaves and then returns, shaking his head. She stays away so long that she is too embarrassed to return. Past the point of no return.

Then that lovely war song begins to play.

I'll be seeing you in all the old familiar places . . .

It is the last dance of the evening and though Peggy wants to be in his arms, wants this more than her next breath, she finds herself sneaking out of the room. Staying in the unlighted places, walking with her head down so no one will try to stop her. Outside in the parking lot she stays as far away from his car as she can. What does she think she is doing? She can't walk all the way home from here.

She hears the violins and the slow, mournful drumbeat. It doesn't make any sense to her but she keeps walking. This is the pattern of her sadness; all her life it has been like this. Some darkness comes over her and then she ruins everyone else's good time and then she is too embarrassed to face anyone so she vanishes.

The road is dark and she is scared. This is what her father was warning her about all those times since she was a girl when he told her that she had to change her attitude. Warning her that her moodiness would bring her trouble.

It has brought her onto a dark road on a winter night.

Of course he came after her. He pulled the car to the side of the road. She felt the heat of the car's headlights on her legs just as he began calling sweetly to her.

If you want to walk then I'll drive alongside you.

This is who he is: someone who will not try to change her or force her to do anything. A boy who accepts her as she is.

When she finally looks up, he is smiling at her. His breath is smoky in the cold night air. He tells her that he was going to ask the band to play "Peg o' My Heart" for the last number. He has already told her that he believes God has brought the two of them together for some purpose. Now he assures her that she can vanish whenever she needs to be alone, whenever the world becomes too sad for her. And he will always be here when she returns. Waiting here for her to look up. *This,* to him, is the meaning of love. And this is easy, waiting for her is easy. After surviving the loss of two brothers, after the long war, the rest of life is a picnic. A cinch.

It was his faith that broke her resistance. He had his optimism and his essential goodness to offer her.

And what did she have to offer him? Her beauty?

Yes, that was it. A young man with a boyish belief in the happiness of life can be persuaded by beauty alone.

In March they were engaged to be married. By then he had convinced her that he was right all along, God intended them to meet. This boy who walked with such purpose and who stood with his shoulders pinned back as if he were still in the army standing at attention and who carried such a fine light in his eyes was a blessing. More than anything else, it was his words that she fell in love with. The way his words always conveyed hope. He seemed incapable of ever saying a bad thing about anyone. One night, kissing her goodbye after a date, he tells her that he has been put on this earth to make her believe in her own future.

Maybe love is a voice. A reassuring voice that becomes familiar and that she cannot imagine never hearing again.

Chapter Twenty-five

A few days before her eighteenth birthday she asked her mother if she could walk her to work at the school cafeteria. She took the same route that she had taken to school every morning, but those mornings now seemed as if they belonged to another lifetime. In those school days she often felt like she was living out ahead of her life a little ways, and she was always waiting for the events of her life to catch up. That morning, though, she could feel her life picking up speed. She told her mother that she and Dick were going to be married. Her mother tried to act surprised but she had already heard the news from Peggy's father; it seems that the word was already out at Lauchman's print shop where he and Dick worked together.

It was going to be a November wedding, the second weekend in November so Peggy could have everyone at her place for Thanksgiving dinner. She had made up her mind that she was going to cook the dinner herself.

After she told her mother this, the two of them burst into laughter. Peggy didn't know the first thing about cooking and her reputation in the kitchen did not promise much of a feast on Thanksgiving. She told her mother that she was going to have to begin giving her cooking lessons.

To Peggy it was already real. The Christmas holidays in her

own place. A tree that she and Dick would decorate together. A quiet Christmas Eve, just the two of them, Bing Crosby and Perry Como singing carols on the radio.

Her mother was happy for her. She already felt like Dick was part of the family. She admired his honesty and believed that he was a young man who would be content with the simple pleasures of life. Like a nice pot roast dinner on Sundays. The first thing that she was going to teach Peggy was how to cook pot roast.

He will make a good husband, her mother said.

The word *husband* hung in the blue stillness of the morning light. A new word for him. A word that now drew Peggy closer to her mother. She was catching up with her and it wasn't difficult for Peggy to imagine the long conversations the two of them would have about cooking and housekeeping and married life. It would be thrilling for Peggy to have her mother as less a mother, more a friend and confidante.

When the school bell rang, the children flew from the playground to the front doors where they tried to stand in long lines. So much energy. Maybe Peggy saw herself walking her children to school when they were small. Or standing at the corner, watching them on the playground with the other kids.

They were shrieking happily as they went inside.

Peggy's mother was worried that she might not have the energy to keep up with the new baby. She had just begun to show and had brought her old maternity clothes down from the attic. Each thing she wore now took her back in time, eleven years in the past, when she was carrying Peggy's brother, Jack. An old part of her life was being returned to her.

Peggy promised to help with the new baby. But her mother

reminded her that she would be gone. You'll have your own place, your own life.

Peggy told her not to worry; she wouldn't live far away, she would see her every day. And the following summer, when her father and Dick began building the house on School Street, the two of them and the new baby would have lots of time together. You can teach me all about babies, Peggy told her mother.

The waiting had begun for both of them. Maybe Peggy could see this. The waiting that would not last long before everything was scattered to the wind.

A goodbye kiss on her mother's cheek. She told Peggy that she hoped she wouldn't have a baby right away. She hoped that she and Dick would have time together first to get to know one another. You'll have plenty of time to have your babies, she said.

Before her mother went inside to work she reminded her that she had packed her lunch; it was in the refrigerator next to her father's. She wanted Peggy to start eating better. All she could really remember seeing her eat in the last two years was her carrot and celery sticks.

Whenever she packed Peggy's lunch like this for her, Peggy dropped it in the wastebasket at the trolley station. Her friend Peg Kirsch caught her doing this. Maybe you should be eating more, she said to her. Peg looked across the table at her in Liedy's one Saturday afternoon when she showed her her engagement ring and she thought how terribly pretty she was. Thin, yes. But not too thin. Her long elegant neck, her high sculpted cheekbones, her dark eyebrows slightly arching. Peg had expected her to go far away from Hatfield. Maybe to become an actress or a model. But Dick was such a sweet boy and she told her that they made a perfect couple.

Peggy was the first friend to become engaged. But even this big step in her life didn't change her reserved nature. Even as she sat there with her friend, showing her her ring, her eyes seemed to be searching for something.

You're the first, Peggy, she said. First to get engaged, first to get married, and probably the first to have a baby!

I want six boys, Peggy said to her friend. And her friend would never forget this.

Winter returned. A bitter cold. Peggy stood outside Lauchman's print shop in Lansdale in the freezing cold rather than go inside. It was a Friday afternoon and she was supposed to meet Dick and her father in the print shop after she finished work at the telephone company. She walked down Broad Street and crossed onto Main at the train station, where she waved goodbye to the girls who she usually rode home on the trolley with. Today was the day Dick was going to introduce her to the guys he worked with in the print shop. She would show them her engagement ring.

She arrived a little early and it wasn't until she fixed her glance upon the front door that she realized she could not go inside. Maybe it was the cold wind that caused her to look behind her just before she reached the door. People moving up and down the sidewalk. Going into the shops and markets along the street. Cars passing. Whenever she looked closely at life this way, she could tell that people lived two lives, the one they showed to others and the one they kept hidden. Or maybe she was the only one to live this way. The only one to see this in the world around her. She was still young enough to believe that no one else on earth felt exactly the way she felt.

In the window of Lauchman's the weekly newspaper was opened to the front page. A headline about that young man they said was a communist. His wife, Mrs. Hiss, was in court now, pleading her husband's innocence.

Peggy walked through the cold to the back of the brick building and stood at the loading dock. Its planked floor trembled through the soles of her feet as the last Linotype press shuddered to a stop. In the silence she could hear the men's voices. All she had to do was walk back to the front door, say hello to Mr. Lauchman, and pass through the swinging door into the shop and smile at everyone. But the longer she stood outside, the more daunting this was, until it seemed like the most difficult thing in the world to do. Why did she want to walk away? What was there for her to be afraid of? And why was she so sad and distant? Was it that she saw something in this life that others didn't see? What was it she saw from the time she was a little girl? Did she see that we are alone? Each of us, despite the busy life swirling around us, is alone. Even a husband couldn't change this.

And what else? What else was she certain of that cold winter day as dusk fell over the afternoon? Just this perhaps, that she was unworthy of anything better than loneliness.

Some of the men had already put on their coats to go home by the time she finally went inside the print shop. Here she is, someone called from the back room. Mr. Lauchman with his wavy hair was already taking her hand. Peggy floated behind him, it was like she was in a dream.

Then she was standing next to Dick, afraid that she would say the wrong thing. Or worse, that she would say nothing at all and that her silence would be misinterpreted. That these men who were her father's friends wouldn't approve of her. And that this boy—*this husband*—would be disappointed with her.

Her father had brought a bottle of beer for each man, to make a toast. A toast and wish of good luck to this girl, and to this boy who would become her husband. *Husband,* a new word for her to say, each time with the weight of a coin on her tongue.

A kiss on her cheek from Dick's good friend Bill Crockett, whose boyish grin she liked so much. Her life was moving quickly now and Bill would be waiting up ahead at two moments when death surrounded her. Could she tell? Could she see something in his eyes?

He joked that day that he had spent the afternoon setting the obituary notices for the weekly newspaper, while Dick, standing at the Linotype press beside him, had set the wedding announcements. You've got all the luck, he says to Dick.

And there she is, her photograph is looking out from the page. It is her high school graduation picture, the one she never liked because her hair was frizzy.

Dick holds the page up in the air. The sound of applause fills the room. And after everyone has wished them the best of everything, Peggy is looking down at the newspaper, reading the words that Dick has set in type one letter at a time. The words that make it all seem suddenly more real than she had imagined it. The words that tell her, Here is your life, Peggy. A new life from which you can no longer disappear.

Chapter Twenty-six

In the photograph of Peggy's wedding shower, her face is less animated than the other girls'. The other girls are opening themselves to the warmth of life; it is her wedding shower, but she is still holding something back. What was it? Was she unsure of her decision to marry Dick? Everyone would remember how completely she fell in love with him. How she spoke of wanting six children with him. Cheaper by the half dozen.

She was unsure of herself, but not of the decision she had made to marry him. He is with her in the photograph of the wedding shower; they are both coming down the basement stairs. He is a little behind her. The girls helped Jenny decorate the room. Paper streamers wrapped around the water pipes. A big cardboard heart taped to the wall. Their names are printed neatly inside the heart—Dick and Peggy.

Jenny gave me the photograph when I went to her house in New Jersey to meet her. I had the picture for several months before I realized that the printing in the cardboard heart matched the printing on the cardboard sign taped below the rear window of the wedding car outside Grace Lutheran Church. It's just a small coincidence, but I wanted to answer as many questions as I could.

I look at this photograph of Peggy with her girlfriends. I have met each of them now, elderly women who must be careful walking in the ice and snow. Two of them lost young husbands in car crashes. One spends the winter in Florida. Their faces barely resemble the faces in the photograph. Peggy is the only one who has escaped the destruction of time. She, who cared so much about her beauty, managed to preserve it in her friends' memories of her.

At the wedding shower they all talked happily about the next decade and the new inventions it was supposed to bring. Electric can openers. Electric typewriters. The whole world plugged in and running on electricity. And colored everything. Colored televisions. Cameras that took colored photographs. Dishwashers. Peggy wanted to know if it would wash pots too. I've never cooked anything without burning the pot, she told the others. And airplanes that went so fast, you could fly to Paris for the weekend. Paris for the weekend!

Someone mentioned that all of them would be turning thirty by the end of this marvelous new decade. Thirty? Yes, thirty, with varicose veins and gray hair.

In the photograph, Peggy's face radiates knowledge; it is as if she is seeing past all of this. Is she thinking that none of this seems real? The future. Maybe this was why she had already made up her mind to have children; she needed children to connect her to the future.

The girls gave her little things for her hope chest. Washcloths and dish towels. Some lipstick for her honeymoon. A record of Don Cornell singing the lyrics she loved so much. *Tomorrow may never come for all we know.*

· · ·

She marked the beginning of summer that year by asking Dick if he would drive them somewhere. Anywhere. Their first trip together. Maybe they would even spend the night. Shock everyone. Why not? She was feeling on top of the world!

Somehow they decided on Lancaster, and Peggy sewed a pale yellow sundress with a bow in back at the waist. It was a hot, sunny day. The upholstered front seat of Dick's car was warm against the backs of her thighs when she got in and she had to sit on her hands until the breeze coming through the opened windows cooled the seat. Dick had a surprise: Mr. Lauchman had spoken with him on payday. He was raising his pay by five cents an hour and he offered to loan Dick whatever he needed to buy furniture and set up housekeeping after the wedding. This meant Peggy would be able to buy the mahogany bedroom set she had seen in the window of Wanamaker's in Philadelphia.

The bedroom set. The kitchen table. The record player. Whatever you want, I'll buy it for you, Dick says.

She is holding his arm with both hands as he drives along. The sunlight is flashing across his face. He fiddles with the radio dial until a baseball game comes on. Something is settling inside her today, some new sense of herself and what she desires most deeply. It makes her feel as if she can see straight through to the rest of her life. It distinguishes her from the people she passes along the highway. They look tired, hurried. Unaware of the world's brightness.

Lancaster is a sea of farmland. Horse-drawn plows turning up the brown soil. In the roads more horses pulling black carriages. On the village green there is a farmer's market. Peggy is still holding Dick's arm with both hands as they pass the displays of needlepoint, the woven baskets. The women's shapeless dresses fall to the grass. The men in black are expressionless. Peggy wonders if they are happy, what is holding them here? She wonders if she could live with nothing as they do. Nothing but love and faith. All of life's material things pouring through her hands. The children are looking up at them. Their faces are white and they stand perfectly still. Peggy wants to take them with her into the excitement and promise of her life.

Dick wants to visit a church. He parks the car and she follows him inside. It is a wooden box filled with summer light. The floorboards are worn through their varnish. Bibles set along the benches like bricks. Dick opens one. The sound of him turning the pages echoes in the emptiness. He wants to read something to her. His favorite passage from the New Testament. So much that he does and says to her is unexpected. Even the sound of his voice at different times can still surprise her. Here it is, he says. He begins to read, but she tells him to stand in front, at the altar. He's reluctant at first but she pushes him on. Then she takes a seat in the front row and looks up at him. Read, go on and read it to me, Dick.

It is the story where one of Christ's followers asks him what it is a good person is supposed to do with his life. Feed my sheep. Tend my sheep. Feed my sheep. Peggy has heard this before, of course. All the years of Sundays are in her someplace. She is overwhelmed with a feeling of contentment. She could live in this sunstruck room. Her life doesn't need to go any farther than this.

Here's my sermon for the day, he calls to her in a rising voice. I love you and will always love you, until the end of time! Amen, he says.

On the ride home she cannot seem to get close enough to

him. She is pressed against his arm like a little child. He tells her that when he was in the army in the Philippines, one of his duties was to bury the food left over after each meal. He thought nothing of it until one day he saw some people digging up the garbage. They were hunched down in the dirt like animals, putting every scrap of rotten food into their mouths. After that he dug very shallow holes in the ground to make it easier for them. It was against orders but he did it anyway.

He raises his arm and puts it around Peggy to draw her closer. She lays her head on his shoulder. He asks if she liked Lancaster, then tells her that he wants to go to college someday. Maybe to the seminary in Lancaster. He asks how that would be for her and she tells him that as long as they are together, nothing else matters. It surprises her how completely she has given herself away to his ideas. That she could lose herself in him so quickly is a little frightening to her. This is the beginning of their first summer together but already it is getting difficult to remember clearly what her life was like before he entered it. This boy next to her is the boy she saw that day on his uncle's porch, helping his cousin Frances walk in her leg braces. He was a stranger to her then. Though not completely.

Chapter Twenty-seven

The hope chest is in her room like a trunk she is packing for some great voyage across the sea. And she is busy sewing right through the summer. The sewing machine is moved up to her bedroom and she is up all hours of the night making dresses. Not just the dresses for the bridesmaids in her wedding, but the dresses she will need as a married woman. She is determined to finish a whole new wardrobe before the wedding. She tells her cousin that she needs to make these dresses now while she is still working at the telephone company, making money to pay for the material. Once she is married she is going to try to have a baby and then she won't have the time or the extra money to sew. She tells her cousin Jean that she's sure she will get pregnant right away, like all the other women on her mother's side of the family, many of whom had twins. Her aunt Edna had three sets of twins!

Peggy's neighbor, Grace Bower, was five years younger but she used to play house with her when they were kids. Grace will remember all her life how her mother told her that Peggy's light was on late, night after night, because she was busy sewing the bridesmaids' dresses for her wedding. Her mother pointed Peggy out to her on three different occasions, three nights when Peggy was sitting at the sewing machine. The first time, Mrs. Bower told her daughter, Peggy is busy making wedding dresses. Then, Peggy is busy making maternity clothes. And, Peggy is sewing baby clothes now.

This marvelous progression in Peggy's life was satisfying to her. There was something up ahead to draw her through the dull hours, something to look forward to. The pale green crinoline dress for her honeymoon is something she can touch, something real that she can believe in. And the long woolen skirt she will wear when company comes to visit her in her first home over the Christmas holidays. She will have people over for dessert, she tells her mother; until she learns to cook, dessert will be fine, and if she needs her mother to bake something for her, she'll be glad to help.

If she has time. Another month and she will have her new baby to care for. It is amazing to Peggy to think that her mother is going to have a baby. Some mornings when she awakens before anyone else in the house, she stands at the threshold of her parents' bedroom and watches her mother turning in her sleep. Each time the baby rolls over inside her, she rolls in her sleep and her hand moves to her belly. It is as if they are going through the steps of a slow dance, learning the timing of each other's moves. In the morning when her mother awakens she will say, I heard you singing again last night while you were sewing, Peggy. I fell asleep again to the sound of you sewing and singing.

Peggy is making the world smaller. In the months before her wedding, her love for Dick is so complete that she doesn't need to go anywhere. He comes to take her dancing and they end up sitting on the couch in her father's house, talking until they can't keep their eyes open any longer. She makes him a cup of coffee before he drives home. While the water is coming to a boil she holds him in her arms. Whatever is happening in the large world outside his embrace doesn't matter at moments like this. All the bad things, all the things that frighten her, are beyond the orbit of her love with Dick.

If she goes anywhere at all it is to baby-sit for her uncle Howard and aunt Muriel. The minute they leave the house with Peggy and Dick in charge of their three small boys, it feels like it all belongs to her. The white lace tablecloth on the dining-room table. The blue ceramic teapot on the kitchen counter. The house. The little boys in their footed pajamas.

All they want to do is wrestle on the living-room floor with Dick. The littlest one is just learning to walk. He wobbles on his feet like a town drunk. He goes through Dick's pockets while his brothers are charging and diving on him. Not so hard, Peggy calls to the boys. Don't pull Dick's hair!

Here is when she falls in love with him as a father. Could there possibly be anything better in life than this? No, nothing. They put all three in the tub together, then read them stories. Tonight Dick is reading to them while Peggy is in the kitchen making him a sandwich from some leftovers in the refrigerator. It's just a sandwich, but before she knows it she has practically every utensil out on the counter. Lettuce everywhere. Dick comes up behind her and kisses the back of her neck. When she turns to look into his eyes the thought that fills her mind is how she will never be able to give him in return what he gives her. What can I give you in return? she asks him.

A sandwich, he says.

No, I'm serious. I don't have anything to offer you.

This is how she feels; next to his goodness, his light, and his childlike faith in her, what can she possibly give him in return.

Yourself, he tells her.

This is all that he wants in the world.

Yes, she tells him, yes, of course he can have all of her; in a moment like this it is easy for her to say it. Easy for her to hold nothing back.

They are silly that night. It is so late when Muriel and Howard come home that Peggy and Dick spend the night there. He sleeps on the couch. At two o'clock in the morning she kisses him goodnight. She has never kissed him this late at night, she tells him. Or this early in the morning.

She lies in bed and makes herself stay awake until three. Then she goes back into the living room and wakes him so he can kiss her again.

This crazy happiness that she is feeling is the happiness that often comes when life is in transition. She is taking a journey to a new destination. Her trunk is nearly packed. It is possible for her to believe that when she reaches this new place, her new life, things will be better there, the darkness won't find her there. It is being nowhere, neither the place where she is nor the place she is going to, that allows her the luxury of hope.

In the morning they are off to Atlantic City. It is Labor Day. Already a chill of fall in the air along the shore. The last of summer. Seagulls huddled in the wind. Peggy rides the blue-green waves, her hair in a pale pink bathing cap. She swims straight out from shore, past all the other swimmers, until Dick calls to her to come back. He looks so skinny in his bathing trunks. She can count each of his ribs.

In sweaters they walk the boardwalk. Holding hands. The shopkeepers notice them the way the world notices lovers. They can see their glances linger. And Peggy and Dick can feel the world's interest in them. It is as if the two of them are giving off a light and a heat that remind others of what they once felt.

In front of an old hotel a long line of wheelchairs made of wicker, painted white. Dick tells her about the wounded soldiers who were brought here during the war. Several of the hotels had been requisitioned by the army. The nurses pushed the sad, broken soldiers up and down the boardwalk in the wheelchairs. Imagine their families coming here to visit them, to see their wounds for the first time. And what about their lovers? Will the wounded soldiers still be loved in their brokenness? Who will love them through a long life?

They leave early with the plan of stopping by the furniture store to take one more look at the bedroom set. But then Peggy decides that she wants him to see the farm where her mother grew up.

It is dusk when they arrive. Coming over the last hill they can see lights on in the farmhouse. Something falls inside her. The bank has sold her mother's farm. It is gone. Somehow she had allowed herself to believe that it would be theirs someday. That they would raise their children here. People would drive by and see her in the tire swing with a small child on her lap. People would envy her life.

At that moment when she is beginning to disappear inside this new disappointment, Dick takes her picture. I have seen this photograph of her. The car is parked along the side of the highway, the fields spreading wide behind it. Peggy wouldn't get out of the car for him. He tried everything but she had decided that because she didn't want to have her picture taken, she was not going to cooperate. Even after such a nice day together at the beach. She has a stern expression on her face. In the day's last slanting sunlight Dick's reflection is caught in the gleaming hubcaps. He is looking down into his box camera. She is glaring past him. A few moments earlier she was pressed against him on the front seat of the car, but now she is a million miles away. His voice is calling to her from another continent, telling her to smile. Smile, Peggy. Please smile. Why won't she give in this one time?

I am told that Dick had the most wonderful, lit-up smile. A quick smile that gave off light. I never saw it myself. I remember him as a man with his head down. When he lost her, he lost his smile forever.

She was hard on him. Her stubbornness is legendary among the people who remember her. They call it that for lack of a better word. Stubbornness. Shall I call it by some other name? Some name that will excuse her? Shall I say that she was prepossessed? Determined? Driven? Do I owe it to her to find the right word that will let her off the hook? Perhaps. But she held this boy's heart in her palm, and she could hurt him deeply.

Peggy climbed over the front seat of the car that day after the photograph and refused to ride next to him the rest of the way home. She lowered her head and wouldn't look up to meet his eyes in the rearview mirror. She knew that she had hurt him again but she could not find her way to apologize.

Chapter Twenty-eight

Audrey is born in early October and Peggy begins getting up even earlier every morning to be awake before the baby. Sewing late into the night, waking early; her days are flying by now. Her time left in this little cramped house on Market Street is drawing to an end. Forty days left. Forty days, after eighteen years beneath her father's roof.

On her way downstairs she stops at her mother's open door and watches her sleeping with the new baby. She stands in the doorway, trying to catch the sound of her breathing. There is the sweet scent of baby powder in the air. The maple-slatted crib is empty. Her mother brought the baby into bed for her middle-of-the-night feeding and she is still asleep between her mother and her father. When the baby is sleeping so peacefully, Peggy cannot pass her without feeling the restless urge to pick her up and press her against her skin. Anyone who ever breathed in the smell of a baby could have invented religion. Once when she was holding her in the first week of her life on this planet her eyes moved in the direction of her mother's voice across the room. So small and new but already aware of the importance of recognizing who is on your side in this world.

This baby is a sister who will always be separated from Peggy by eighteen years. How many times she had asked her mother for a baby sister when she was a little girl herself, all those years when she and a new sister might have become close friends. Her mother's hair was turning gray by the time she finally got pregnant again. In church the pious ladies drew their heads together and whispered when her mother passed them with her swollen belly out in front of her like someone pushing a wheelbarrow. All of that has only drawn Peggy closer to her mother. The church ladies were concentrating on the next life while her mother was living out the mysteries of this one. Peggy took pride in it, the warm knowledge that some passion had survived in her mother, a passion that connected her to one of life's deep desires.

On one of those autumn days Peggy and her father put up a longer clothesline, one that reaches from the back door of the house to a corner of the little garage in the alley. Since the baby arrived he has been talking about building the house earlier; his original plan was to start the next spring, but now he is thinking about starting right away. With the new baby and grandmother and grandfather living in the tiny house, there is barely room for him to move. No place for him to be alone in his own house. He has begun spending more time in the garage with his tools, which he keeps in perfect order. He is a man with three children now. Someone has told him that once there are three, once the mother and father are outnumbered, everything changes, the operation of the family becomes a full-time job.

Peggy understands his feelings of claustrophobia and she feels bad to be contributing to the clutter in his house. Last night she finished another bridesmaid's dress; she and her mother worked on it together in the kitchen. Peggy stayed up long after her mother went off to bed because she wanted to finish cleaning up so that when her father got up in the morning he would be able to have his breakfast in a tidy kitchen.

This morning after he has finished with the clothesline he tells her to come to the garage, he has something for her. He is walking ahead of her with his head down. He looks so sad and small to her, getting smaller it seems. There is no way for her to reach him. She will never know who he really is, only the superficial things that he cares about. A clean house, a waxed car, his tools in their proper place on his workbench, the flaps on his shirt pockets ironed so they don't stick out. Maybe at the end of a life these are the things we remember best about a person. These little things contribute to an ordered world. And she shared with him the deep desire to impose some order upon the world. In this way she is her father's child and always will be. She could never be less like him, more carefree, one of those people who drop their clothes on the floor and leave them there. Like Dick. This is something else she admires about him; the material world is of no consequence to him. Except for his precious car, you could strip him of his possessions and it would take him a few months to figure out that he was missing anything. She will be picking up after him all her life, she knows this, though she doesn't know why it is she cares. These little habits of hers, lining her shoes neatly in her closet, folding her clothes at the end of the day, maybe these are the things someone will remember about her someday. More than her ideas or her passions. Because she keeps those ideas and passions and fears carefully concealed behind an ordered world.

Her father has a pair of chopsticks for her. He has taken a pair of drumsticks that he had in the garage, planed them down and sanded them. She had mentioned the other night that she wanted to try Chinese food for the first time on her honeymoon in New York City and that she wanted to learn how to use chopsticks before the wedding. So, here you go, Peggy, a set of your own chopsticks. Her father doesn't know the proper way to hold them, she'll have to ask her uncle Howard about that, it is a skill he picked up during the war.

She thanks her father. He bows his head again. She should take two steps across the space dividing them and kiss him. Maybe put her arms around him. But she doesn't. Instead she takes the chopsticks up to her room where she wraps them in a blue-and-white-checked dish towel and places them in her hope chest for the life that will begin before too long.

There was always laundry to hang out that fall, and as the days turned toward winter, the cotton diapers turned stiff as they dried. Peggy sets them over the heating grate in the kitchen to thaw. Her baby sister's clothing is no bigger than doll's clothes. The impossibly small T-shirts and socks, proof of the long life we have on this earth. People are forever saying that life is short, but hanging out the baby's laundry confirms something that Peggy may have already suspected is true, that we travel a long way in our life.

Hanging out the laundry is reassuring. It is an elemental and sensible act that places her in the company of every other person on the earth who is caring for a baby. And everyone who has ever cared for a baby. It is not hard to picture her grandmother Swan hanging her mother's baby clothes in the wind that blew across the cornfields on the farm that is now gone. And her mother hanging out hers. It is an act that allows Peggy to see the deep patterns in life and for this reason she does it slowly, never hurrying to finish. And neatly too.

She is a person who hangs all the diapers side by side, then the T-shirts, then the socks. A neatly hung load of laundry is satisfying to her. It's silly, she knows this, but she can't deny that it brings her pleasure. In the backyards up and down Market Street, people seem to be in a silent competition to keep the neatest life. You can see it in the way they care for their lawns as well. It seems that ever since the men came home from the war, order has taken a central place in people's lives. Order to counteract the terrible disorder, the unspeakable disorder of the war.

An ordered life. Could she sense that all this order is merely an illusion that we hold on to so we don't have to face the fact that we are barely clinging to this planet? Had she already learned that life can be thrown into disorder almost at any moment? Is this why she tried to make everything so neat in her little world?

It was a way of managing her fear.

She was afraid of the airplanes that crossed the skies while she hung out the laundry for her mother. So many more planes in the skies this late autumn of 1949. They were from the airfield at Willowgrove where fighter pilots were being trained for the next war, which is never far from her mind now. No matter how many times Dick tries to convince her that there won't be a war in Korea, she is unconvinced.

One Saturday morning when she was supposed to be waiting for him to pick her up to go shopping she went to the library instead, and left word with her mother to tell him to meet her there.

When he came through the library door he was smiling and wearing his new tennis sweater, the one she would always say she loved to see him in—off-white, with a red and a blue stripe along the V neck and around each cuff. She will show him on the atlas where this country is. Korea. So small, it disappears beneath her thumb. But on the other side of the world.

He is dumbfounded.

How can you keep thinking about these things, Peggy?

What things?

All the things that make people sad.

There's no answer to this, and so she doesn't even try to explain. She is supposed to go look at the house on Broad Street in Lansdale this morning, but somehow she has forgotten this. How could she forget this? How could she forget that the way to overcome her terrible fears is to give herself up to the momentum of a normal life. To let herself be carried along by the currents of a real life.

It's a fine little house, a row house along a wide street with overhanging elm trees. There are stairs up from the sidewalk to a front porch. Each house has its own porch, sectioned off from the houses on both sides by a scrolled handrail. At the top of the stairs in the house next door, and in the one next to that, is a baby gate. There is a lot of life in these little houses, and she can hear it faintly if she listens. She will never be alone here. If she cares to, she can invite the young mothers over for coffee. She can set the table with the cups and saucers she has chosen for her wedding gifts. Desert Rose pattern.

It is exactly like the row house Dick lives in with his parents just a few blocks from here. Looking through the front windows into the living room she shows him where she wants to put the Christmas tree. He counts the rooms for her, and tells her there's an extra room.

And there, he says, turning to face the street. There's

the hospital right there. The Elm Terrace Hospital is just across the street. It's where his sister, Jean, had her baby boy last week.

In the backyard, a long rectangle leading to a tiny garage, a clothesline was already hung. It was raining that morning or she might have seen the wives who would become her neighbors hanging out their laundry up and down the street. A room for a baby. A backyard with a clothesline. If she brings a baby into this world, she brings with it the routines and duties that can fill her life and distract her from her distant worries. Her life will be reordered around the necessity that only a baby can provide. She will be far too busy to worry about the airplanes in the sky above her.

Dick has something to show her this morning. A small card that he has printed at Lauchman's.

Dick and Peggy Snyder
will be receiving guests
after December fourth at
623 North Broad Street
Lansdale, Pennsylvania.

He has already paid the first month's rent. In four weeks they will be living here together. The wedding already behind them. Christmas lights on the tree. And maybe a strand of lights across the railing of the front porch.

Holding the card in her hand, she begins to feel it is all becoming real to her.

Chapter Twenty-nine

She looks up just as she is leaving the church. There is her father with a box of rice raised above his head. And then the rice showers over her. She is wearing a white cloth coat over her wedding dress, holding up the long train with her left hand. Her right hand is on Dick's arm. It is a cold gray day. A shadowless day. Her mother looks very old, and there is a troubled expression on Peggy's face. No one can remember ever seeing a prettier bride. Maybe she is overwhelmed by everything, maybe this explains the faraway look in her eyes. She is there, but not really there, in the photograph. Her mind is on something else.

It is dark by the time they make their getaway from the reception. She and Dick dance a slow dance to "Peg o' My Heart," the only couple on the dance floor, then they are off to New York City. One of their friends gives her a small package wrapped in gold-foil paper on her way out to the honeymoon car. In the excitement of the day, with everything she and Dick have to talk about during the four-hour drive to New York City, they forget all about the present until the night is over and Dick is asleep beside her for the first time and she cannot seem to close her eyes. She would always remember the happy faces, and often recall them; more than anything else, she wanted people to have fun at her wedding, and it seems they all did. They were all smiling when she turned with Dick to walk down the aisle as man and wife. And now, on her wedding night, with her husband asleep next to her, the memory of this day is enough to reassure her of the promise of her life. All the people at the church had been drawn into the orbit of their fine *new* life. You could see it on their smiling faces.

She turns on the bedside light and opens the gift wrapped in gold-foil paper. A best-seller, *Cheaper by the Dozen.* The true story of a family with twelve red-haired children.

Life is a pair of glasses folded on the table by the bed, the morning's first light glancing off their gold rims. Life is someone's clothing draped over the arm of a chair with her own. The boy she loves lying beside her is the confirmation of life's order and holiness. A thin gold band on his finger that matches her own. His face on the pillow. We see who a person is in the world if we watch him waking. Those first seconds as they are returning from sleep, before they remember where they are in the universe. This is a boy who asks for nothing for himself except that she never leave him. A pledge she cannot imagine breaking. There are his polished black shoes on the floor by the door. Sometime in the night an ache she carried inside her since he first touched her, a longing that she learned to accommodate, finally disappeared, replaced by a marvelous lightness. Across the room a shelf slides out of the wall to make a desk. On a piece of stationery marked "Taft Hotel," she writes him a note and places it next to his face on the pillow. Are you as happy as I am?

Here she is on the eleventh floor of a hotel in the world's largest city. It seems strange. And yet, because she is still young enough to look behind her and see clearly the path that led her here, life feels like it is in her control.

She has brought far too many clothes. Four suitcases full. And a hatbox. She packed like a movie star. One suitcase for each day. Like an actress who must change for every scene.

Maybe she would prefer if I didn't write about this, about how she cared about her beauty. Her nails and lipstick. Her complexion. She attended to her beauty. With dresses, she was partial to a bow or sash at the waist or collar, something extra to make the costume complete, so she could hide behind it. But here in New York City she is free to show her face, to stare at everyone who passes. It is the first time in her life that she is standing in a place where no one knows her and there is no one she has ever disappointed! She can be anyone here. It is enough to make her go skipping down the sidewalks.

For five days Dick can barely keep up with her. The deal is if he can catch her, she will kiss him before she runs off again. Kiss him at the Statue of Liberty, on top of the Empire State Building, in front of the department stores on Fifth Avenue, their great sidewalk windows decorated for Christmas. Opening her eyes while he is kissing her, and there she is reflected in the glass. Who is she? A girl with a pair of chopsticks in her purse. A girl who once dreamed of living in this city. A girl in the arms of a boy who loves her depthlessly. She can feel his love for her, a trembling that rises off his skin. The only thing she has to do in the world now is lean toward him, return his touch.

In the hotel lobby, a woman named Miss Allen sits at a desk and answers tourists' questions about New York City. She is famous, she tells them; there is no question she cannot answer. She wears her gray hair pulled back in a bun. The first time Peggy walked through the lobby Miss Allen stopped her and said, Honeymoon, right? I can tell. Each time she sees Peggy, she smiles knowingly at her. A woman's secret perhaps? Memories of her own honeymoon. It makes Peggy wonder how she looks to her. It makes her feel sorry for her and for everyone on earth who is no longer young and in love.

There is a drugstore in the hotel. Two dining rooms, two nightclubs, and a florist where Dick buys her a bouquet of roses. He is holding them behind his back when he steps off the elevator right into her arms. She pushes him back inside and when the doors close he leans her against the wood-paneled elevator wall. It is the first elevator she has ever been on. She kisses him all the way down. When the doors begin to open, she can feel him pulling away. But she isn't going to let him go. For some reason she wants everyone to see her in his arms.

I saw him just last week. Peggy's young man, my old father. I watched him sleeping in a chair, his soft white hair pushed to one side. His hands folded in his lap. We were talking about their honeymoon. He was telling me that they both chose the Taft Hotel because there had been a weekly radio broadcast from its rooftop dance club, big-band music which the two of them listened to every Saturday from the time they first met. The Vincent Lopez band. I was listening to my father and watching his expression; I could see something in his eyes, some spark of recognition. But then he bowed his head and fell asleep. My little boy, Jack, came up to me and whispered in my ear, Does Granddad fall asleep all the time because of that thing in his head?

I wasn't really listening to Jack. I was watching Peggy's husband in his sleep and remembering that he always slept with a tormented expression on his face that is so unlike the look he showed to the world when he was awake. He never appears to be resting in his sleep. As a small boy I used to stand beside him as he slept in his gold-colored chair in the living room where he always fell asleep reading the newspaper after he came home from work. I watched him carefully as a child. For the longest time before he remarried, I thought he was my brother. I remember when he went out at night with his friends, I'd be at the front door crying for him to stay home and he would promise to bring something back for me. And no matter how late it was when he returned, I would be awake, waiting for him to keep his promise. He never let me down when I was a child. He always made me feel like I was special to him. He always took my part. He was always for his boys. I would like to tell Peggy this.

But when he was sleeping his face frightened me; he always looked like he was pulling against a powerful force. When I saw him the other day I realized that in the last forty-seven years, Peggy's death always inhabited his sleep. I don't think he survived her death. The boy who jitterbugged on the rooftop of the Taft Hotel vanished when she died.

Chapter Thirty

On Peggy's first shift back at the telephone company, the other girls want to know all about her time in New York City. They gather around her at the end of the day while she tells them about the big fantastic world beyond the small boroughs of Pennsylvania. Even as she is answering their questions, she is aware of the unlikelihood that *she,* a small-town girl whose life up until now had been lived within two square miles, would ever be speaking of her travels to distant places. Looking into their faces, listening to the excitement in their voices, brings her a sudden contentment because her life seems finally to have found its proper course. For so long now she never felt a part of the world that everyone else occupied, and now at last she occupies a different world.

The girls have heard that she'll be working only half-day shifts now, and they want to know if this is true.

Yes, it's true.

Oh dear, bread and beer, if I was married, I wouldn't be here, one of them sings with a great, jealous sigh.

Peggy's life has opened to her. Of course the world is full of married ladies, some of them even newly married like her. But all of them put together couldn't convince her that her life with Dick wasn't going to be extraordinary in some way. She can feel this deep in her bones.

She is going to work the noon-to-five shift from now on, so she invites them to come see her apartment at 623 North Broad Street on Saturday morning.

Six twenty-three Broad Street? One girl teases her about this. Peg, that's just across the street from the Elm Terrace maternity unit!

Married lady. Up early, standing at the gas stove burning bacon. Dick comes bounding into the kitchen; he thought the place was on fire.

No, it's just the bacon. It's the stove's fault. I'm used to an electric stove, but this damned stove with its gas flame keeps burning the frying pan.

Dick tries everything to make her laugh. He reminds her that it isn't even five o'clock in the morning, it'll be hours before any of the girls show up. He wants her to come back to bed with him.

She can't, not now. Not until she has figured out this ridiculous stove.

When the girls arrive, there are four pans soaking in water in the sink and all the windows are opened to clear the air. They tease her, and she smiles for them, pretends to laugh it off. But that night she is still angry about it and when Dick tries to console her, she won't speak to him about it. It is very late when she sits down at her sewing machine to try and calm herself. A new dress she's been working on is folded on the chair next to the machine. When she picks it up it smells like bacon grease. She buries her face in it; it's enough to make her want to weep. She will have to go through her life smelling like a short-order cook. Before she throws the dress away, she makes herself take out every stitch with a pair of scissors. One stitch at a time. It takes most of the night.

She was too young to understand why she was so hard on

herself. She was only eighteen years old, and it was 1950, a time when most people didn't speak of anything that wasn't simple and pleasant. But she was tortured by her unworthiness, which was proven to her over and over again in each failure and every time she disappointed someone. Her inadequacies were so disgusting that the world deserved the chance to be rid of her. Her friends deserved the same.

And what about Dick, whose love for her was so blinding that he couldn't see her failings? His love for her was the deepest thing in his comprehension. He loved her with the unconditional love of a child.

And she knew this. On the good days when she could see past her own terrors, she knew this.

Count the good days she had in her little apartment on Broad Street, the days before the unraveling began. What about Christmas, her first and last Christmas? She sewed two stockings out of corduroy material and embroidered their names with white thread. She sent letters to her friends, inviting them over for the holidays. She imagined how she would dust and vacuum and scrub the place so that it looked just right, just the way she wanted everything to look when her friends came over. When she couldn't sleep, and when her eyes were too tired to sew, she just walked from room to room, rejoicing in all of the promise of her life.

BOOK FOUR

Chapter Thirty-one

It is just after midnight and my son, Jack, is on the floor beside my bed, inside his sleeping bag. When he was three and four years old he slept in our bedroom every night, and now that he is nine and we are in a larger house, he has his own room for the first time and I can't remember the last time he slept beside me like this. The reason he is here is that tonight was hockey night for me, and I took him along to the rink because he wanted to watch me play.

I'm a goalie, or I once was something of one, but with a crushed disk in my back, it's been five years since I played in a real game. Tonight was my first time on the ice in a long while, and the truth is, I needed Jack with me to help me get into my goalie equipment because I can't bend over and reach the lower buckles on my leg pads.

On the drive into Portland I was thinking about how my father used to go to all my football and baseball games when I was in high school and how I used to love to hit home runs and score touchdowns for him. When colleges began writing to me offering me scholarships, I remember feeling like I was coming into my own as a man at last, and that one of the things I was going to do all my life was take care of my father. This was before a neurosurgeon in Williamsport, Pennsylvania, told him he had a brain tumor and told me in the hospital corridor outside my father's room that the tumor was the size of a lime and needed to be removed.

I argued with my father a long time when he decided that he was going to surrender his illness to God and to the healing power of his faith rather than have surgery. This had made me angry at first until I woke up to the fact that it was his life.

His faith has held him up for a long time now. He has done well, though his faculties have been gradually diminished. He had been a marvelous driver, I always felt safe in the car when he was behind the wheel, but now it has been years since he drove.

I've been thinking about this all day today and it is the reason I said yes when the call came from the men's ice hockey league asking me if I could play in the goal tonight.

I was nervous driving in. The last time I had played in a real game I wasn't concentrating the way you have to with a puck sailing at you. I let one get past my glove and when it struck me on my Adam's apple, it cut off my oxygen and I passed out.

I wasn't afraid of getting hit tonight, though. I was afraid of letting Jack down.

I won the game with Jack standing just behind me, behind the glass, watching every save. I don't think I ever played better. I took off my helmet and watched my son out of the corner of my eye when everyone on the team skated to the net to shake my hand after it was over.

In the locker room someone passed around cans of beer. I'd stripped off half of my equipment when a guy on skates appeared in the doorway. The next game was about to start and they were short a goaltender.

I had to get my son home to bed, it was a school night. I gave that excuse. But Jack said it was fine, he wasn't tired and he always got too much sleep at night anyway. He had already begun to take my pads out of my duffel bag. The guys in the room were watching us, smiling. One of them threw me another beer. Jack put his arm around my shoulder and said, "My dad will play."

As soon as I got on the ice I could see that these guys weren't "B" level players. In the warmups the pucks were flying past me, there was nothing I could do to stop them.

But Jack was there watching and I won because he was standing behind me and because I had a couple of strong defense men skating in front of me. I made the big saves when I had to.

Now he is asleep on the floor beside me and I feel *privileged* that he wanted to stay near me tonight instead of sleeping in his own room. And there is something else; I played the second game of hockey tonight for another reason. It wasn't that I didn't want my son to think I was getting old; he knew I was getting old before I even put my skates on. I just wanted him to see that I was still strong so that he wouldn't be afraid to push me when he thought I needed to be pushed, to yell at me and to stand up for himself when I was being unfair. He knew I was getting old but I didn't want him to have to *worry* about me.

I have brought my family with me to Pennsylvania. We are in a room at the Holiday Inn in Kulpsville just off the turnpike. Everyone was exhausted from the trip and fell asleep right after dinner. It is seven o'clock, not even dark, and I am looking around this crowded room at my family sleeping so peacefully. How long ago was it that my children learned to fall asleep so easily? There were years when getting the children to sleep was the biggest challenge of my life. Those years are gone. It hits me now how fast those years disappeared. I wonder how Peggy would have coped with me and my brother when we were small on the nights when we couldn't fall asleep. The nights when she was so exhausted that she would have gladly traded away four or five years of her life just to finally reach the point when we could put ourselves to sleep.

It's a hot night like the Pennsylvania nights I remember from my boyhood, the time of year when the wool baseball uniform I wore in Little League would stick to my neck and shoulders.

I am sitting in bed, thinking how, in a few days, my brother will arrive and he and I will go to knock on Dr. Wright's door. Then, for the first time since Peggy's death in 1950, the five men in my nightmare will be assembled. Dr. Wright, my grandfather, my father, my brother, and I. I will have my answer. I will know if we conspired to steal my mother's life from her.

After a while I get up to take a walk. The six of us are packed into this room and I have to move my oldest daughter, Erin, who is sleeping on the floor, in order to open the door. The rest of the children have scattered their clothes around the room, but Erin's things are set neatly on a chair next to mine. Everything is carefully folded, and beneath the chair her tennis sneakers and her shoes are lined up beside my own, the toes all the same distance from the inside legs of the chair.

Erin is twelve years old now and, like me, she will stop to straighten a painting on a wall or to wipe the kitchen counter on her way out the door. She likes things neat. She won't say much to anyone about her feelings; she has gone to see the movie *Titanic* three times with her friends this winter but she has not spoken to her mother or me about what keeps drawing her back to that tragedy. She carries everything deep inside her. I have a picture of my mother at this age standing in the church choir; her face so closely resembles Erin's that you have to look again to be sure. And like Peggy, this daughter can sing like an angel. Amy Oliver, who worked at the telephone company with Peggy when they were both seventeen years old, has told me that men fell in love with my mother because of her voice. This is why the bookie fell in love with her.

I lift my daughter from the floor to lay her in bed next to Colleen. When I carry her, her arms go straight out at her sides, as if she is flying through the night. I want to enter her sleep. I want to know why she takes the time to put her clothes away at the end of each day. I want to know why this matters to her.

A few miles from here Peggy's aunt Anna lives on Columbia Street just three blocks from the house on Market Street where she was born and married. She remembered going to visit Peggy in her Broad Street apartment soon after she and Dick returned from their honeymoon. Peggy had just finished taking a bath, and before she would speak with Anna she had to clean the tub. Anna waited in the living room a long time and then went down the hall and found Peggy finishing and then starting in again to scrub the same place in the tub that she had already cleaned.

I don't know what this means but it is on my mind as I walk outside and cross the hotel parking lot. I am thinking of Peggy who is buried just a few miles from here. I am sorry that it took me this long to acknowledge her and to bring my family to stand at her grave.

Not far from where I'm standing there is a dogwood tree in full blossom. I walk toward it with the thought that I will break off four small branches, one for each of my children to lay at Peggy's grave tomorrow. When I am standing below the branches a strong gust of wind comes out of nowhere. I can hear it charging across the parking lot so low to the ground that I can only feel it on my ankles as it picks up bits of paper and gravel. Then suddenly the wind races up through the branches above my head and a storm of white petals from the dogwood tree showers over me, filling the air, and covering me like snow.

It is the shock of it that leaves me shivering and I know that I must talk to my father. There is something I must say to him. Tonight, before the morning comes.

It takes thirty minutes to drive there and all the way over I am thinking that the wind in the branches of the dogwood tree, like the double rainbows in the sky on my first trip to find my mother, belong to a spirit that marks her presence in the world.

And this is why I am yelling at my father. This is why I am telling him that he should have taken me to her grave years ago. He is standing in the kitchen in his pajamas and it comes into my head that my daughter Nell asked me recently about my mother's wedding album. She wanted to see their wedding album and I had no way of knowing what had become of it, or if there had even been a wedding album.

My father has a soup spoon in his hand because he wants to make me something to eat.

"I'm not hungry, I already told you, I'm not hungry."

"That's okay then."

"It's not okay, Dad. Nothing is okay! Don't you see that?

Can't you see anything? All my life I've been tiptoeing around you because I was afraid to make you upset. Why didn't you ever take me to see where she was buried? Before . . . *before* you got the stupid tumor in your head. Because now I can't even yell at you about it, I can't swear at you or tell you that you let her down, because you might fall over right in front of me, and then what the hell will I do?"

He didn't say a word. He just sort of drifted down the hallway toward his bed while I was yelling at him that it was all on his shoulders because he had sent me the photograph of him and my mother in the wedding car.

"My obligation is to her!" I yelled at him. "I don't owe you anything. I don't owe you silence! And what happened to the rest of the pictures of my mother, what about her wedding album? You must have had a damned wedding album."

When I finally stopped he was standing inside his bedroom doorway, looking out at me. "Do you still hear Peggy's voice when you write in the mornings?" he asked me softly.

"What?"

"You told me that you can hear Peggy's voice in the morning," he said again.

I think of it as the worst night of my life. I'm sitting outside on the front stoop of the apartment house. I can't go back inside and I can't go back to the room at the Holiday Inn where my daughter has lined up her shoes.

On the ground in front of me there are three white petals from the dogwood tree that must have fallen off me on my way up the steps.

I can't go back inside because I'm afraid my father will fall into one of his seizures, and I'll be to blame for it. I remember then how the doctor who first diagnosed his brain tumor asked me if I recalled my father ever telling me that he'd been struck in the head when he was growing up. Some trauma from early in his life.

"Nothing I know of," I had said to the doctor, though I was thinking, *He took a hard blow to his heart.*

"I believe God will heal me," my father had told the doctor.

Now I am trying to imagine him assigning my mother's illness during her pregnancy to the same God, the same power of faith.

This faith of his, where had it come from? How had he kept believing in God's generosity after losing his twin brother, and then another brother and then his wife?

His brother's coffin lay in the living room of the rented house in Skippack for two days before the burial. For weeks after his death my father rose from his bed at night when he heard his mother crying in her grief. He stood outside the door to her bedroom, sometimes for hours, until she had stopped crying and he was sure that she was sleeping.

I am thinking about the time I took him swimming in the ocean off Martha's Vineyard in big waves that were running ashore on a riptide after a storm. This was before the tumor, the last time I ever saw him healthy and fit. We were riding the waves onto the beach at dusk. You had to catch them just right, laying your body out flat just behind the curl as the wave was breaking, or the tremendous force would crush you headfirst against the rocks and sand.

I saw him lining up the wrong way in front of a wave that was cresting high above his head. I yelled to him just as he went under. I saw him swallowed by the wave, just the white bottoms of his feet sticking up out of the boiling surf. I began swimming toward him and yelling for him but the riptide was dragging him away from me. When I finally reached him, he was on the bottom and didn't have the strength left to lift his head out of the water.

Now I wonder if he was already returning to my mother when I caught hold of his arm and pulled him out of the sea. He had finished his job by then; my brother and I turned twenty years old that summer.

And was he trying again to return to my mother when he wouldn't allow the neurosurgeon to operate? Was he waiting for God to sweep him away to wherever his two brothers and Peggy had gone before him?

I was still on the porch of the apartment house when the paperboy arrived. I could see that he was afraid to get too close.

"I'll take it," I said. I put the newspaper under my arm and watched him turn away. He was walking across the grass when I called to him. The words came out before I knew that I was saying anything. "Do you know the man who lives here?" I said, pointing to the set of windows on the ground floor.

I was pleased when he stopped and turned to look back at me. "Not really," he said.

"I'm visiting my father here. He was a paperboy when he was about your age."

He didn't seem to know what to say to this so I waved once and he hiked his bag of papers up higher on his shoulder before he went on walking. I looked at the apartment house. All the windows were the same, and the doors were the same, and I suppose all the people living there were the same to the boy who delivered their newspapers, and I guess I wanted to give him some small reason to care about my father.

It was Sunday morning. When my father appeared at the door he was already dressed for church in a white shirt and a tie.

As soon as I saw him smile at me I knew that he was going to ask me to go to church with him. And though I could have talked my way out of it, I told him I would.

The church was maybe ten miles away. We were driving through the rain on a narrow country road and when we rounded one corner there was a car overturned in the ditch just ahead of us. A woman was standing in the road, holding her face in her hands. I pulled off the road and got out and ran up to her. She was shaking and when I asked her if she was hurt she said that she wasn't but that there was someone still inside the wrecked car.

I crawled down into the ditch. It was very quiet and I was aware of birds singing in the trees above my head. I tried to see inside the car but the glass on the windows was shattered. The doors were jammed shut by the collapsed roof. I pushed my knee against one window and when it fell into pieces, I smelled gasoline and I saw a young girl hanging upside down. I was amazed when she turned her head and looked at me calmly. She told me that she was unhurt but she couldn't get the seatbelt unhooked. Then she began crying faintly.

I crawled in through the window and cradled her head in my arms while I tried to get the seatbelt to release. I tried everything and then told her that I was going to have to leave her to go find a knife or a pair of scissors to cut the belt. She began to cry louder, and I can't explain this, but suddenly when I looked at her face it was Peggy's, the same face that I had seen as a young boy. I was holding my mother's head against my chest. She was helpless and scared.

Someone slid down into the ditch beside us. I called out that I needed a knife. I kept holding the girl in my arms and thinking how helpless my mother must have felt when she learned in January 1950 that she was pregnant. What must have come upon her was the realization that being pregnant is a public matter. Her anonymity was gone. There was no place she could hide from the world. People were watching her, asking her how she felt. Waiting for her and wishing her well. Expecting her to smile and be happy.

"It's as sharp as a razor," a man said when he handed me the knife.

The seatbelt was so tight against her stomach that I couldn't slide the blade of the knife beneath it. "Take a deep breath," I said, "and don't let it out until I've cut you free."

I stared into her eyes and I knew in that moment that my father was not to blame for Peggy's death. Neither was my grandfather or her doctor. I was responsible. And I was the one who had never asked my father to tell me about her.

Even after I cut the seatbelt and pulled the girl from the car and carried her up the embankment to the road, I was still thinking that it was Peggy in my arms. I didn't want to let go of her when the ambulance arrived.

Chapter Thirty-two

No company came to visit Peggy and Dick that Christmas. Just before the holidays she became sick. A stomach flu, a cold in her stomach is what she thinks is wrong. It is worse each time she tries to eat something.

The nausea is bad enough to wake her from her night sleep. She stands alone in the kitchen, vomiting into the sink while moonlight falls on her toes. It is January of 1950, the start of a new decade. Ten years ago she was nine years old, a girl playing jump rope. The silly song she sang while jumping is still in her head:

> Fudge, fudge, call the judge,
> Peggy's having a bay-bee!
> Wrap it up in toilet paper
> send it down the elevator,
> Boy!
> Girl!
> Twins!
> Triplets!

By the end of the next ten years she will be turning thirty. Some nights she sits in a chair, listening to the radio. The news is terrible. The United States government and a committee of scientists are studying the feasibility of building a hydrogen bomb one thousand times more powerful than the Hiroshima uranium bomb. Forty-two women die in a fire on the psychiatric ward of the Catholic Mercy Hospital in Davenport, Iowa. Barred windows hampered rescue. Doors locked from the outside prevented escape ... Alger Hiss (there is that name again) is convicted and sentenced to five years in prison.

Her breasts are sore. The soft circles around her nipples are turning the color of chocolate.

The day before her doctor's appointment, Peg Kirsch is supposed to stop by, to see the apartment. At the last minute Peggy asks her to meet her in town instead because she hasn't felt well enough to vacuum. Dirty dishes in the sink, an unmade bed; as she glances around the rooms they don't seem to belong to her. She never imagined herself in rooms where things were not put neatly away.

It takes an effort to dress and Peg wouldn't mind if she didn't bother to brush her hair, but this will be Peg's first glimpse of her since the wedding and she wants her to see that she is happy, that she has made the right choice, that her life is fine.

They buy candy bars at the Nut Shop and then walk to Memorial Park to watch the deer. Across the way children are feeding them through the fence. How wonderful to have deer in the center of town. They imagine these children dreaming of the deer tonight.

Peg will remember this day because of the dark circles around her friend's eyes and because she looks so thin. Peggy makes a joke of this, telling her that it is difficult for two people to survive on whatever is not burned to death when she cooks. She asks Peg if she is still homesick at nursing school. Yes. Her father keeps telling her to just come home, but her mother is still adamant.

Peggy tells her that she is envious of her relationship with her father.

She asks Peggy about Dick, and Peggy replies that he is sweet to her, so patient and understanding.

Her friend will remember this almost fifty years later; she will recall how happy Peggy seemed as she described Dick.

They say goodbye at the trolley. They set a date for the next Friday night for Peg to come over for dinner, and on her way back to the nursing school at Grandview Hospital, the thought comes into her mind that Peggy might be feeling sick because she is pregnant.

When Friday comes, Peggy is still throwing up almost everything she eats and so she calls her friend and cancels dinner.

A cold in her stomach is what she has been thinking is wrong with her. But when her family doctor, Paul Moyer, suggests that she may be pregnant, it is as if she has just walked around a corner straight into a door. She is angry at herself. Until now she didn't know that it is possible to feel both blessed and stupid in the same breath. How could she not know?

She declines Dr. Moyer's offer to fit her in on Friday for an examination and tests to confirm his suspicion. It only takes a small lie on her part to turn him away, and so she tells him that she'll return to do the tests next week after her stomach feels better.

Then she goes home alone and waits for Dick. There is time for her to think through the implications of this. She will never be alone again once she has a baby. She saw her mother surrender her life to a new baby. This will be *her* now. She might be summoned at any moment. She will not be able to hide from the world any longer. The cry of an infant will call her out into the open.

She never returns to Dr. Moyer's office. Instead she sees a physician on the other side of town. His office and examining rooms are on the first floor of a large house. His name is Dr. Edward Wright, a distinguished physician, precise in his manner, highly regarded in the small medical community as brilliant, a little distant, perhaps even slightly arrogant. But exceedingly gifted at his work.

His nurse wants to know why Peggy has decided not to stay with Dr. Moyer. Peggy says the easiest thing to tell her, that she is living just across town from here and for the sake of convenience she decided to come to Dr. Wright. The truth is more complicated and none of her business anyway. The truth is that Dr. Paul Moyer has known her since she was a girl, he has taken care of everyone in her family and was her mother's doctor just a few months before when her sister, Audrey, was born. She wants her own doctor, someone who will see her as a grown woman.

The exam itself is an invasion that she has been dreading since the first time Aunt Muriel told her what was involved in having a baby. It makes Peggy feel like her life has suddenly fallen from her hands.

It's good news, the doctor tells her. Congratulations, you're going to have a baby.

She is off the ground for a few moments, thinking of all the people she must write and tell. In the next room the nurse is checking her urine for protein.

When Peggy is dressed, Dr. Wright tells her about a book

that she should read: *Answers to Your Questions About Pregnancy and Childbirth.* He writes the title down on the back of one of his cards. Read it, he says. And pay attention to the sections which explain a condition called toxemia. He doesn't want her to worry, but there are traces of protein in her urine, and her blood pressure is high for a nineteen-year-old girl. These two things are the reason he tells her that she might want to plan on having her baby at the Sacred Heart Hospital in Norristown. Ordinarily he would expect to deliver her baby at Elm Terrace, which is right across the street from where she lives, but if the toxemia does present itself, it could result in complications, and Sacred Heart is a far better equipped hospital.

Not to worry, he says at last. He is just being careful. Now go celebrate with your husband, he's going to be a father. And read the book.

She is staring at his hands when he gets up from behind his desk to show her to the door.

A wife is supposed to surprise her husband; at least this is what she has seen in the movies, so she buys the book in town before she returns home. Where will she leave it for him to find? On the bedside table? In the empty bedroom that will be the baby's room? Next to the sewing machine?

She decides on the kitchen table where they eat their meals. The tin table painted with white enamel paint. Next to a tall blue candle in a crystal vase that was once her aunt Lilly's. Then she sets about cooking Dick's favorite meal. Brook trout which are not easy to find in January. Her mother knows the proprietor of a market in Telford.

So, then, trout, mashed potatoes with lumps that she can't

ever seem to get out, and carrots. She makes him take a shower first. When he steps out of the bathroom she is dressed—high heels and a pale blue cotton dress with a dark blue bow; the four thin strands of pearls that he gave her for Christmas. He takes her in his arms.

She lays her head on his shoulder.

So, this is who I am, she is thinking. I am a man's wife. A child's mother. That is how I will find my way through this life.

She is hungry by dinnertime. Has she ever been this hungry before? She eats everything on her plate and then runs to the bathroom and throws it all back up. Oh Peggy, she can hear Dick calling from the kitchen.

Standing at the stove she fills her plate a second time. When she sits down at the table, he asks her what he can do to help. I'm going to make myself eat all this food, she tells him.

A second time she throws it all back up in the toilet.

So she gives up.

When she tells him, he is overjoyed with the news. So soon? So soon? Could she be wrong? He reaches across the table and takes her hands. The bones of her wrists are so thin and frail that he says he is worried she might not be strong enough to have a baby. Don't be silly, she tells him. You never saw me play field hockey.

In the morning she will go shopping for more material. All the married-lady dresses that she sewed must now be put away to make room for the maternity clothes she will make. And then the baby clothes. Aunt Lilly will tell her to make neutral things, clothing that either a girl or a boy can wear. But Peggy won't hear of this, and she buys the patterns for little boys' trousers. Proper trousers, she calls them. Her mother and her aunt laugh at this. For almost a year all the baby will need is pajamas, they tell her. But this is her baby and she will dress him properly. *Him.* Even in this first month she is sure her baby is a boy. Even in this first month the baby is real to her. Only to her.

Chapter Thirty-three

On a sunstruck morning my brother meets me at the Holiday Inn in Kulpsville. I have a map and I've marked the road where Dr. Wright lives. He doesn't know that we are coming. In my shirt pocket I have the index card from the Elm Terrace Hospital with his name and signature below Peggy's name and the word *preeclampsia*.

My brother is driving slowly down Main Street, pointing out where the hobby shop used to be, recalling how when we turned ten we were finally allowed to walk there by ourselves from our house just three-quarters of a mile away. I can show him things he has never known before: Peggy and Dick's brick walk-up apartment on North Broad. Lauchman's print shop where Dick went to work every day. The telephone company where Peggy worked. The train station where the trolley from Hatfield came in. "Why didn't we ever know these things before?" he is saying. "I've learned more about our mother in the past few months than in the rest of my life."

On Clearspring Road we stop in front of the small stucco house with green trim. One pane of glass is missing from the garage windows. The willow tree reaches high above the roof now. Our bedroom window facing north is where I always imagined Peggy came in on the nights she visited me. "You never heard her voice?" I ask my brother.

"No."

Why had she spoken only to me? Because I was the weaker of her two sons. I was the one who would hide from the world as she had, and in life's deep loneliness there would be, at least, her voice to accompany me.

This is the house we moved into a few days after Dick remarried. Another wedding. A new bride. Of course my mother would have been curious to see.

At the end of the street, the silver water tower we walked past on the way to school and back each day. Its high chain-link fence with barbed wire around the top. We threw stones at the tower, and by the time we were in the third grade we could reach it and it would whistle back a kind of shriek when the stone hit.

The elementary school which was brand-new in 1956 is now showing signs of age. Streaks of rust along the window trim. Cracks in the concrete foundation. We drew pictures at our desks when the first astronaut rode into outer space. The teacher collected them and put them in a metal box that was buried beneath the building's cornerstone for the demolition crew to discover in the distant future when, we believed, people would be living on the moon.

In the basement below the cafeteria with its wood-and-gray-steel chairs is the fallout shelter where we practiced our escape from a Russian bomb. I think of it now and am reminded of the bomb shelter that Peggy saw being constructed. Rows and rows of Campbell's soup cans.

She missed the crazy years, and the bad years. She was dead

before the exquisite order and hope of these neighborhoods died away completely.

We count the numbers on Leslie Road. Then pull off to the side.

There is a front porch on the house, a swing hanging from the rafters. The grounds are manicured, the grass is freshly cut. We ring the bell and stand in silence. Dave is looking up at the blue sky. "Beautiful day," he says. He is facing this calmly and I am glad to have him with me.

Not a sound from inside the house. Through a window, I see the rooms are without light. It seems that we have come on a day when he is gone.

But then the door swings open. I can see the wariness in his eyes. So I smile and say we are Peggy Snyder's twin sons. "We've gotten old. I'm sorry."

When I put out my hand he shakes it vigorously and tells us to come in.

He walks ahead of us into the living room. My brother and I sit together on one couch, then stand when his wife appears. She is wearing a starched white blouse and a long wool skirt. He is dressed in a coat and tie as if he is expecting to see patients.

"We're just trying to get to know who our mother was," I tell him.

"I never knew her," he says. "I delivered over a thousand babies and I never lost a mother."

"Yes," I say, "you told me."

"I've gone over and over my records and I never had a patient by that name. The only thing I can figure is that I must have been called in to deliver you, that's all. I must have been on call, covering for your mother's doctor."

I ask him where he referred his difficult cases in the early 1950s, women facing difficult pregnancies.

"Sacred Heart in Norristown," he says. Then he apologizes again for not remembering anything. "I checked my records and your mother wasn't my patient."

I feel my heart beating faster against the index card from my mother's hospital bed in my shirt pocket. Then I ask him if he has children.

"I have a daughter," he says.

We listen to him and his wife as they speak of this fine daughter. The doctor remembers her IQ and I am watching his hands, thinking how they reached inside Peggy. His face is severe, such a stern look. She would have found no refuge looking up into his face. He is a man who would have sized her up as not terribly bright, from an uneducated family. Someone headed for the dull gray working-class life. Nothing as exceptional as the life of his daughter.

My brother is asking again if he will get in touch with us should he remember anything. I just want to get out of the house.

"Where was your office?" Dave asks.

"Derstein Street."

My father is waiting at the motel. I put my arm around him and ask him one last question. "Where did you take Peggy for her regular visits to the doctor when she was pregnant? Can you remember where the doctor's office was?"

"Yes. Derstein Street," he says.

He is certain of this. And in the days that follow I grow more sure that Dr. Wright has lied to me. He is a man who remembers his daughter's IQ but not the first set of twins he delivered, not the only mother who ever died in his care?

Everyone in the medical community at the time of Peggy's death still remembers, except Dr. Wright. And he never asked my brother or me a single question about her. This is what makes me so certain he is lying. Not to ask one question. Where did your mother die? Who raised you boys? Is your father still alive? Nothing.

I wish I could have made him remember my mother. I wish I could have told him what it was like for her in the end. How she felt herself slipping away into madness, trying to recall the words to that record by Don Cornell, anything from a better time, something to pull herself back to this world. Her horrible headaches, her skull pounding to the noise from the racetrack in Hatfield on those hot August nights when sleep wouldn't come. The engines of the race cars ripping and screaming through her consciousness. And all her worst fears exploding in her mind on June 25, when the war her husband promised her would never come, began. Three days later the army of North Korea had taken Seoul and over the radio came word that World War II veterans on active reserve status would be called to fight. That day W. Stuart Symington, chairman of the National Security Resources Board, told the American Red Cross that a foreign power had the capacity to attack all of the United States for the first time in history. "We have no adequate defense against such an attack," he warned.

Chapter Thirty-four

The pregnancy book Peggy is reading in February to prepare herself for having a baby suggests daily exercise. It
claims that the pain and discomfort of labor will be reduced
by being in good physical condition. She decides to start
taking regular walks around the block. She takes them in the
evening just before going to bed, with the hope that she
will be tired enough to fall asleep without a long struggle.

On one of those February nights, as she is passing the
Elm Terrace Hospital, two young men come dashing down
the sidewalk like burglars being chased. One of them is trying
to button his long overcoat as he is running. It brushes
her legs when he passes and she turns to see where they are
going.

They run right up the front steps of the hospital and throw
open the big door. Light from inside spills out across the
porch. And brings with it the most ungodly scream that she
has ever heard. Even when the door closes the sound is barely
diminished. It is inside her. It draws her to the porch and up
the first step. The woman screaming on the other side of the
door will one day be *her* in her labor. She knows this. And the
two boys who were summoned here tonight by a telephone
call, boys who belong to the volunteer corps, will carry the
mother in a stretcher up the stairs to the delivery room where

a doctor, maybe *her* doctor, is washing his hands in the enamel sink.

It is enough to stop her heart if she lets it. The fear of this night becoming *her* night is something she cannot ignore. She can either sink beneath it, surrendering the last of her strength to its force, or face it head-on with the defiance of a young, beautiful girl whose body is strong and growing stronger. This defiance is a kind of faith, isn't it? The faith to say I know how terrible the storm may become, but I have the strength to ride through it. God will help me ride it through with the strong heart that he has given me.

Dick is bringing home boxes from the print shop. Boxes that she lines with tissue paper. She is packing away the married-lady dresses. Three to a box. She is down on her knees wearing a slim blue skirt, a pale blue silk blouse. She is folding the dresses carefully. Her husband is watching from across the room. Smoking a cigarette. Trying to smile. Halloween, he says at once. By Halloween you'll be unpacking your wonderful dresses.

She is on her knees, making an elaborate ceremony of this. What makes her husband's smile disappear? Can he feel the time draining from this moment? What makes him walk across the room and kneel down next to her and take her in his arms as if she were going away on a long journey that might take the rest of her life?

Peggy is sitting at her glass-topped vanity combing her hair when Eileen Crockett calls on the telephone to ask if she can come over. Her husband, Bill, is at work with Dick at the print shop and she has just gotten off work at the hospital. I'm not dressed yet for the day, Peggy tells her. Give me an hour, Eileen.

When she arrives Peggy is still in her nightgown, still brushing her hair at the glass-topped vanity in her bedroom. The sound of her knocking at the door brings Peggy out of what feels like a trance. This is the second or third time she has had this happen in the past few weeks and it's embarrassing to her. This morning Eileen is solicitous, apologizing for disturbing her. She is a tall, dark, and beautiful girl, a nurse like so many of Peggy's other acquaintances, and when she first sees her standing at the back door off the kitchen, her impulse is to tell her what has just happened, how she was so lost in a daydream which she can no longer recall that an hour and a half somehow slipped away without her moving even a finger. Like she was hypnotized.

Eileen has a present for her wrapped in silver-foil paper with a thin red ribbon. Open it, she says.

It is another book about pregnancy, this one by a Dr. Benjamin Spock. Eileen is in a rush to tell her what a marvelous new book it is, she's been urging every pregnant girl she knows to read it because it makes such good simple sense of the whole business of having babies and caring for them. All the expectant mothers who are patients of the doctor she works with are reading it. Anyway, she says to her, Happy Birthday, Peg.

Birthday? How could she have forgotten that today was her nineteenth birthday?

Eileen will remember this: how Peggy tried to conceal the fact that she had forgotten, but it was clear to Eileen that she had. And it will worry her. She will speak with her husband about this, and he will tell Dick. And when Dick asks Peggy about it, she will tell him it was nothing, nothing at all. It will start a small argument between them, and she will lose her patience and walk out of the room, leaving him standing there with his hands open at his sides, trying to reason with her.

Her nineteenth birthday. The news is not good. Albert Einstein is on the radio news, warning the country about the H-bomb. If man succeeds in making the hydrogen bomb, radioactive poisoning of the atmosphere and hence annihilation of any life on earth has been brought within the range of technical possibility. And in a six-hour speech, Senator Joseph R. McCarthy, the Republican senator from Wisconsin, has renewed charges that fifty-seven communists have been employed in the State Department.

What kind of a world is she bringing a child into? This is on her mind on her birthday. The fear that she might not be able to protect this child in America's future.

She is alone in the bedroom again, sitting again at the vanity. Sometimes when she loses her patience with Dick, she can find her way back to her affection for him by recalling their wedding day. The white lace covering the backs of her hands. When she looks down at her hands today, the flesh around her gold wedding band is swollen. Staring at her hand makes her heart race with worry; her long and elegant fingers which always pleased her and which inspired her across the last few years to diet continually, have disappeared. Their elegance is gone. The thin elegance she always thought she was hiding behind like a cat hiding behind a blade of grass. Now her hand looks like a starfish. The fingers are fat and misshapen. It is a hand she has never seen before. And she stares at it with contempt because . . . she cannot say exactly why. Maybe it is just that these pudgy fingers are not who she is. She is so delicate and pale that a friend of

Frances (remember Frances over on Cherry Street, in her metal braces, paralyzed from polio?) has described her as a "Dresden doll."

I keep telling her that she has to eat for two now, Dick says as he turns to glance at her in the back seat of the Chevy. He and Bill Crockett are in front. Peggy and Eileen are in back. They are heading to Atlantic City for the day because this is how Peggy wanted to celebrate her nineteenth birthday. It's a cold winter day, much too cold to be at the shore, and they have all teased her about wanting to make this trip. But once Peg makes up her mind to do something . . . she heard Dick say on the telephone when he told the Crocketts of her plans.

Once she makes up her mind to do something, no one can dissuade her.

Eileen, the nurse, tells her that the old notion of eating for two isn't quite true. You should just eat good nutritional meals, regular portions. And you should expect to gain maybe thirty-five pounds. With your delicate frame, perhaps even as little as twenty-five.

Eileen is sweet, but this is the part of being pregnant that Peggy cannot stand. The public nature of it. There she is in her *condition*. And everyone believes they are qualified to comment about her *condition*.

Why are my fingers swollen when I'm not eating anything at all? She doesn't ask this question, but it runs through her mind as she stares down at her hand.

Maybe you're eating for three! Dick says. She can see a smile light up his face. I was a twin. There are two sets of twins on my side of the family, and one of Peg's aunts had three sets of twins herself.

Well, I hope they like crackers, she says. She has a box of Saltines on her lap and she is eating them one after another, slowly, chewing each one fifty times before she swallows, the way Aunt Anna told her to. She has heard that morning sickness can be cured by always keeping something in your stomach. The crackers do seem to be helping today.

The world sails by outside the car window. Long, even fields and then rolling farmland giving way to scrub pines and the salt scent of the sea. Dick and Bill are talking about the communists in Korea, discussing the chances for war there. We are going to have to take the commies on somewhere, Bill says. It might as well be Korea. Better than here, at home.

The giant billboard on the right-hand side of the road, a puppy pulling down a little child's bathing suit in an advertisement for Coppertone sunbathing oil.

There are so many Chinese communists, they say we'd run out of bullets to gun them all down. We wouldn't be able to make new bullets fast enough to kill the yellow hordes.

Peggy asks them to please stop. Eileen is looking through the pregnancy book which she has brought along to show her. Listen to this, everyone, she announces. She reads the part about the first cells dividing. The cells in salt water. You are carrying an ocean in your belly.

And listen to this, boys. How does the ideal husband behave during his wife's pregnancy? First, last, and always he remembers he has a bigger share of the responsibility than the mere launching of the performance at one end or the paying for it at the other. He should be cheerful and patient—

That's me! Dick sings out.

—relieve his wife of worries, avoid quarrels—

We never quarrel, do we, sweetheart?

—cater to her desires (up to the point where she is merely trying to be mollycoddled), overlook her appearance—

You look beautiful to me!

—and take an interest in their impending acquisition. Any expectant father who accomplishes all this deserves a Congressional Medal.

Pin it on right here, will you, Peg?

From behind she puts her arms around him and lays her head on his shoulder. She kisses his cheek and whispers, Pearls, pearls.

As far as maternity clothing is concerned, Eileen reads on, your clothing should be comfortable, but also attractive to your husband!

More laughter. The sound of it is reassuring. The pale sky is flying past Peggy's window. She can feel herself smile. When are we going to get there, Daddy?

The laughter rises, such a sweet, sweet sound. And she rolls down her window to let the salt air fill the car. A smell as sweet as the sound of laughter.

But there is her hand again, her pudgy fingers; isn't this the lousy way it always is with her and the world, always the collision of her desire to be at peace with the world, to laugh and smile and to embrace the miracles in her midst, her beautiful friends here with her, and her devoted young husband, and her baby growing inside her. But always, just as she is reaching to embrace all of this, there is something more to be afraid of, and to run from.

She doesn't want Dick to turn and see, so she puts her hands beneath her thighs and sits on them the rest of the way.

. . .

On the shore they are teasing her—Whose kooky idea was it to come to the beach, anyway? They have to shout to be heard above the wind which is driving in, straight off the sea. It is the kind of weather that makes Peggy feel like she could be swept off the face of the earth in an instant without anyone even realizing that she is gone.

But it feels so good to be near the sea. This is the place where she fell in love with Dick. He and Bill are walking ahead. They still look like boys, not yet men, though they have been to war. Boys really. Slugging each other playfully. Peggy gathers a handful of small stones and surprises Dick by running up behind him and pouring them into his pocket. I don't want you to blow away! I'm weighing you down so you won't blow away!

There is the Steel Pier up ahead where the horse and rider dive from the top of a seventy-foot platform into a pool of water. In New York City on her honeymoon Peggy met a woman who had seen this on *her* honeymoon and she told Peggy never to go see it because it was terrifying for the horse. Peggy has never been able to forget this, the horrible image of a horse falling headfirst.

She takes Eileen's arm and leans close to speak into her ear. The sight of Dick and Bill ahead of her has made her feel certain one more time that this baby is going to be a boy. I want six boys, she tells Eileen, but if I can't get that many, I want at least two to take the places of the brothers Dick lost when he was a boy.

This is the only person she will ever tell.

On the ride home in the back seat Eileen answers some of her medical questions. Your doctor has said no salt because of your high blood pressure which can aggravate the toxemia. Toxemia can be dangerous. In extreme cases it is called preeclampsia, and can be fatal. Trust your doctor and do whatever he tells you, Eileen says.

That night after Dick had fallen to sleep, Peggy put her long winter coat on over her nightgown and walked out onto the front porch to see if she could hear any sounds coming from the labor room of Elm Terrace. The second floor was dark but she stayed outside and watched for a long time, waiting for a light to go on in the delivery room and for the boys from the volunteer service corps to come dashing down Broad Street, waiting for a baby to be born on her birthday.

But nothing broke the darkness of the night.

Chapter Thirty-five

I should conceal this truth. I should turn my back to some of the things that my mother did so this will be a more uplifting story. A story that people can nod their heads to. I should say that Peggy went blithely along, believing in God and fearing nothing. It would be a story about faith that people read again and again when they are blue and when they catch an unexpected glimpse of the truth about their own lives—that they, like Peggy, are only barely hanging on to this life, that a single telephone call can throw our careful lives into unspeakable disorder. I should not say that sorrow awaits us all.

I can just say that Dick went off to work each morning whistling, which is the truth—the neighbors remember this. A skinny young man in khaki pants walking down the cement pathway to his green Chevrolet, whistling. Happy because he had such a beautiful girl for his wife, a girl he never dreamed might be interested in him, a kid who still had pimples on his face and who had false teeth issued to him by the United States Army on his fifth day in boot camp.

I should hide the fact that in April, at the beginning of Peggy's fifth month, there was already enough concern on her doctor's part that he advised against the trip to Washington, D.C., that she and Dick were planning to take with Roy and

Naomi Meyers. The afternoon of her office visit, Dr. Wright's nurse called Dick at Lauchman's print shop. You're not letting your wife eat salt, are you?

My father remembers the doctor forbidding Peggy to eat salt. This is one of the few things he can recall through his amnesia.

And I can write this now because it is also true: This is the only thing he ever knew, the only thing he was ever told about her sickness. Peggy hid it all from him.

Aunt Anna smiled wisely at me when I laid out my theory for her as we sat in her living room on Columbia Street where she spends her days caring for her husband. I told her that I had this nightmare about the five men conspiring, on religious grounds, to force my mother to keep her baby.

"If you had ever known your mother you would understand that no one ever could have done that to her. Peggy made up her own mind to keep you boys. You were real to her. Remember that. To everyone else you were not yet real. And she never told your father about any of it. She made her choice and kept it all to herself."

My father went off to work whistling each morning because no one ever told him how sick Peggy was. She never told him that during her exam the day before the trip to Washington, the doctor explained that by the end of this month if her condition continued to deteriorate she was going to have to give up her baby because the baby was poisoning her. He believed in taking every precaution. He was a skilled physician and he had never lost a mother.

There is a doctor in Lansdale who was in high school with my mother, one class ahead. He called me in April to say he needed to speak with me. He told me that he might have been in love with Peggy from a distance, though she never knew he existed. She was the most beautiful girl he had ever seen and when he was away at medical school and learned that she had died, he told himself that one day he was going to find out exactly what had happened.

Five years after her death he returned to Lansdale to begin his medical practice. On a rainy afternoon he looked up her medical records at Grandview Hospital. He began asking questions discreetly and he found that it was common knowledge among the physicians on the hospital staff that Peggy Snyder had died needlessly. Her doctor, Edward Wright, had done everything within his power to persuade her to give up her baby. But her mind was set, she refused to listen to him.

The doctor invited me to his house for breakfast. He stood at the stove cooking omelettes and telling me everything he remembered. She was young, she had that going for her, and Dr. Wright might have held out a slim hope. But in the early morning hours of August 11, when he delivered Peggy's baby only to discover that there was a second baby inside her, he knew that it was hopeless.

He said that a man like Dr. Wright would have washed his hands of my mother after she refused to follow his warning. And now when Dr. Wright says that he never had my mother for a patient, he believes he is telling the truth. Peggy pushed him out of her life just when she needed him most. He was her last chance to survive.

"When I say she died *needlessly*," he told me, "I mean she could have lived if she had been willing to lose you and your brother."

. . .

She kept it all to herself. She made up her mind because to her alone we were already real.

But she was angry too. Her swollen hands made her angry. And her swollen feet and her face which was gradually becoming unrecognizable to her.

She was angry at the headaches that woke her from her sleep, and she was angry at her husband who said the same thing over and over when he laid cold washcloths on her forehead to try to numb the pain. You'll be all right, Peggy, just don't put salt on your celery.

It was the only thing he knew to say to her.

She wanted to see the cherry blossoms in Washington. She had gone to the city two years earlier for her senior class trip in high school and she wanted to return just to see if it was as beautiful a city as she remembered it. Were the monuments as white under their night lights as she remembered them? So white they appear covered in snow.

They were beautiful and she was happy and would never forget standing in moonlight before the Lincoln Memorial. And Arlington Cemetery with its rows of white crosses for as far you can see. Identical white crosses that look like sugar cubes on the distant hillsides. Standing there with Dick, she finally knew what the war on the radio had cost.

But she was angry and distracted the whole trip because the doctor had also told her that in another month, six weeks at the most, if she was still determined to keep the baby until its full term, she was going to have to be cared for for the remainder of her pregnancy. She was going to have to move back into her father's house on Market Street and spend the next three months in bed. Back in her father's house where the progression will fall from her life, the marvelous progression of the past twelve months when she went from being a single girl to an engaged girl to a married woman to a pregnant wife. She can't imagine what she will *do* each day in her father's house. Or how she will find any room there to be alone.

After her return from this trip to Washington she locks herself in her room all day for two days while she takes out all the seams of her maternity clothes because they have become too tight. She has a small scalpel as sharp as a razor, with a tortoiseshell handle and a slightly hooked blade. She cuts the seams one stitch at a time, the anger making her hand into a fist around the scalpel. She won't speak to Dick for these two days because now the marvelous progression which took her from being a high school girl to a pregnant wife feels to her like it has stolen something from her. She didn't even have time to learn what it meant to be a wife and now she is going to have to learn what it means to be a mother. And a fat lady too. A fat lady in her father's tiny half house on Market Street.

But in Washington she recalls her high school trip here. How she could have been kissed by Lawrence Jackman standing in the shadow of the Bureau of Printing and Engraving where they had watched money being made. And in Arlington Cemetery she ends up lying in the grass in her husband's arms. Surrounded by so many dead men. Dead husbands and fathers from the war. All of this was happening while she was learning how to walk in high heels and wear her hair like Ginger Rogers. And it makes her feel stupid now. So stupid. How could she have ever believed that the war was heroic rescues and parades and illicit love affairs. The war wasn't at all what it had sounded like on the radio. The war was death. Countless graves. With her husband's arms around her, one pale cheek pressed against his shirt collar, she sees the white crosses at ground level spilled across the green fields, each one commemorating a fiancée, wife, and mother whose world has stopped.

Dick tells her that he, too, has the right to be buried here because he is a veteran. This she does not want to hear. So she kisses his lips to make him stop talking. And he leans harder against her, and she tells herself that this is something she will never again take for granted. This chance to be touched and to touch someone she loves before the time comes for that person to be swept away and hidden forever beneath the grass.

It is raining hard all the way home. Dick is driving; thin curls of smoke from his cigarette rise above his head and explode silently against the roof. Roy talks about a story he has read in *Reader's Digest:* in Great Britain, the government has commissioned the nation's most talented artists and sculptors to work with veterans whose faces were disfigured in the war. A castle somewhere in England has been requisitioned by the government. This is where the artists and the soldiers live. Many of the soldiers have hideous wounds. Their noses have been shot off, their eyelids are gone. Each soldier arrives with a photograph of how he looked before the war, then the artists work on making him an identical mask that will conceal his wounds.

Dick is asking how the masks stay on, how they are attached. Peggy leans her cheek against the cool glass window and looks down at her puffy hands. Something like despair rises through her body. Oh God, how will she ever pass through another hour of her life without thinking of those boys with their noses shot off? How will she ever escape the image of these boys? It is an unspeakable horror and she is certain that it will happen again, there will be another war.

Why must she be married to a man who can't see this? How can he keep smiling, and why is it that nothing can extinguish his optimism?

When Roy is finished explaining that the masks are held on by glasses, Dick begins to extol the virtues of the United States government which has made so many opportunities available to its veterans of war. College tuition, which he is going to take advantage of one day. And the loans to buy a house. He makes it all sound so wonderful and each time his voice rises with enthusiasm, it makes Peggy want to scream. Why can't he see that everything is going to come crashing down? Why can't he be with her in her despair?

She knows the answer to this because she has invented it herself: if he were standing beside her in her despair, she would take him down with her and he would not be waiting with his smile to light the way back for her to return. Yes, this is why she must thank God for his cheerfulness and his faith. She must be grateful and she must never do anything intentionally to deprive him of his pleasure in life, or his hope. She must never tell him anything that might extinguish his light, the light that leads her back to his love for her. If there is another war she must fall into his embrace like one of those wives in the photographs in *Life* magazine. And then bravely surrender him to the ship or the train that will carry him away. Let him keep smiling through her misery and fear. He's a boy in love with life. And the worst thing that she could ever do is give him a reason to doubt life's goodness. She must keep her fears hidden. Hide them deeper and deeper inside her until she can feel the physical weight of her sorrow, and loneliness is in everything she knows.

Those two nights in April she has all her maternity clothes from her closet piled on the tin table in the kitchen. Dick is sleeping while she sits through the night tearing out the seams. She is trying to slow her mind so she can think clearly, but everything is crowding behind her temples, each thought catching on something inside her head and playing itself over and over. GENERAL ELECTRIC. The words on the refrigerator. She keeps seeing these words even after she has turned back to the dress in her hands. She is tearing the dress apart but her mind is speaking these maddening words! GENERAL ELECTRIC. GENERAL ELECTRIC. As if there is some deep meaning to these words, as if these words hold the truth about the rich and varied love that she and her husband have shared in their brief time together. She can't turn away from the words and they won't let go. She is memorizing the curling letters in those words outlined on the refrigerator door while the blood is thickening behind her eyes and the headache begins again with a cold spark at the back of her neck. Maybe she shouldn't have gotten married so soon. Her mouth feels dry and scratchy. And there is some sound behind the door in the kitchen that leads to the basement. A scratching sound like the sound of a small animal trying to gnaw its way through the door. The sound is growing louder and the hole is closing above her head again, the concrete lid to the bomb shelter is being screwed down tightly on top of her.

Chapter Thirty-six

One night in Maine I could hear my mother's voice so clearly that I wrote this long letter to her.

I can see you on one of those warm May days, taking out the storm windows in the brick apartment and washing them before you put in the screens. Washing each window with hot water and soap. Scalding water that turns your hands red, your hands which were once so delicate, the nails strong and ridged with perfect white half-moons. By now your fingers look like sausages. Dick keeps telling you how his sister, Jean, gained weight with her first baby, and you listen to him and you try to believe that he is right, that there is nothing to worry about. And you hate yourself for making a big deal of your swollen hands because in the scheme of things, with people starving in the world and with families still mourning the loss of loved ones in the war, your troubles are small and inconsequential. But still you can't look at your hands without thinking that you are becoming disfigured and you need a way to hide from the world like the British soldiers who will hide behind masks for the remainder of their lives. You are scrubbing the windows until your hands are raw, the skin on your fingers cracked just short of bleeding; it is a kind of punishment, and you can hear your mother whispering to your husband, "She'll get through it, she's my daughter, I know how strong she is."

Your mother has been calling you every morning, offering to come by and help you pack up your things so you and Dick can move into their house on Market Street where she can wait on you hand and foot like your doctor has advised. But how can you go back to your father's house? The little half house which is already so crowded with your baby sister and your brother.

Maybe if you keep busy you can dissuade them from this plan. Maybe if you can show them that you are able to clean the windows yourself and put in all the screens, then they will give up the idea that you must move back home and be cared for like an invalid.

Maybe you can persuade them to leave you alone. How? By smiling?

Yes, by becoming the perfect picture of a housewife. Dressed with your makeup on and your husband's breakfast on the table before he awakens each morning. And standing at the door to greet him at the end of the day, dressed in a different outfit, smiling. Hello sweetheart, I made meatloaf for dinner.

And macaroni and cheese. You spend two days teaching yourself how to make macaroni and cheese. And at night after supper when you sit out on the back porch with Dick, you keep smiling even when the sky is filled with bombers from the Air Force base at Willowgrove and the radio is talking more and more of the troubles in Korea.

Keep smiling. And what about a double date this Friday night with Tom Pugles, Dick's buddy, and Shirley Graham, the girl Tom's dating now. *Cinderella* is opening at the Strand and you're going to catch the early show and then have dinner together.

But when the night comes you make Dick call Tom and change it to the late movie and no dinner. And you insist on meeting them at the theater. Inside the theater. In the dark because that afternoon you looked through the Landsdale High School yearbook and saw how pretty and how thin Shirley is. Just the sight of your hand next to her smiling face on the page is enough to make your throat go dry.

But you keep trying. Joking with Tom that as soon as you have delivered this baby you're going to hit him up for a ride in his state trooper cruiser. You want him to promise that he'll flash the blue lights and drive as fast as it will go!

The macaroni and cheese in the glass casserole pan is for Dick's sister, Jean, and her husband, Page, who you invited to dinner the next night. You are trying again to show your husband that you can manage. You have worked all day to get it right, washing every bowl and pan that you dirty as you go along so that there is nothing in the sink or on the counter that will be evidence of your struggle. When you bend over to pick a wood-handled spoon up off the floor you are a little short of breath. It's nothing really, it's only the strangeness of the feeling that draws your attention from the world of preparing meals and entertaining guests, back to the world of yourself. Inside yourself. You can feel the darkness cover you as you lean against the counter, the strip of metal trim around the wood counter pressing against your belly. If you lean harder, it disappears in the soft folds of skin that were never there before. Close your eyes and stop this before it claims you. Concentrate on something else. Concentrate on the picture of the sweet nurse who you have met, the woman who will help deliver your baby. Anna Hartman. Remember how she smiled at you when you were introduced to her the other day? Her strong handshake and her fine bright eyes? Can't you see her handing you your baby—Here's your son, Peggy. Congratulations. And the first thing you'll do is count all the fingers and toes like every mother does. And take a good, long look at his face to make sure you'll never forget it.

No one remembers today what it was that happened, Peggy. Jean and Page arrived just a little before Dick had returned home from work. They brought their new baby, a son named Douglas, nine months old now, just learning how to laugh at the world. They sat him on the burgundy-colored couch between them. He was dressed in short pants and a white T-shirt like the ones your father wore to the print shop. Ditchdigger T-shirts you called them. Everything was fine until he began crying hard about something. You watched Jean hold him up in the air and talk baby talk to him until he calmed down. And then you excused yourself and went into the bedroom. You closed the door behind you and sat down on the floor and leaned against the door.

This is where you stayed for the rest of the night. When Dick called to you and pleaded with you to open the door, you leaned your weight harder against it and told him that you felt too sick to come out. You wouldn't let him in.

Even while it's happening you know exactly how terrible this evening will be in everyone's memory of it. But you cannot stop what is happening. Twice during dinner, Dick, like a child, comes hopefully to the door and knocks gently. I just can't, you say to him. You can hear the plates and silverware. Before Jean and Page arrived you had set the tin table with your fancy wedding dishes. The beautiful hand-painted Desert Rose plates. The matching cups and saucers. They aren't speaking a word over dinner. It is so terribly silent that you can hear them chewing. You can smell the smoke from their after-dinner cigarettes.

Finally when their baby begins to fuss, they say goodnight. The screen door closes behind them with a slow sigh. And then it begins again. Your husband's hopeful tapping on the bedroom door. You'll feel better in the morning, Peg. He says this all the time to you now, and you are trying to remember when he first began to say it.

Somehow you fall asleep leaning against the bedroom door. When you wake, it is the middle of the night. Broad Street is deserted. No cars go by. You wake suddenly, startled by the silence around you. There is a narrow band of light on the floor beside you coming from the light on the stove that Dick has left on for you.

You find him sleeping on the couch, his feet hanging over the end, and when you kneel down beside him and lay your head on his chest, he shudders and whispers to you that he doesn't ever want to stop trying to make you happy but he is scared now. He's scared that he may give up on you. He's scared that he may lose his faith in you.

He begins to cry. This is the first time you have made your husband cry. (This you will now have to carry with you.) The sound of him struggling to speak through his tears is enough to take your breath away. He is trying to tell you that he is scared and you are trying to stay where you are with your face pressed against him while the top of your head is burning and you begin to drift away. And the last thing you want to do is leave him behind. All you want is to stay where you are, right next to his sorrow, and so, to keep yourself from flying off, you try again to picture the center of your childhood town. To walk the streets in your memory, going calmly from store to store in Hatfield. Hirzel Drug Store with the glass vials in the window, and Anders Market. Beans Grocery and the old Knipe Hotel.

On Mother's Day I took my family to your grave for the first time, Peggy. I stood beside Colleen, watching our children. Erin pulled the weeds that had grown up around the marble stone. Cara asked me if I was going to be buried here when I died. Nell did a cartwheel in the grass, pretending this was not a sad place. Jack buried a quarter and said, "Someday I'm going to come back and see if it's still here."

I wondered what would be left of you. A mat of hair, your shoes. Pages from the Bible your mother buried with you.

I tried to remember the times in my life when I felt close to you. The time I was caught in a gale in a small sailboat, two miles from the harbor. I was alone, down on my knees bailing the boat and trying to hold it on course. I had my St. Christopher's medal between my teeth and I was talking to you as I am now.

And in 1987, when Colleen and I had gone to spend the winter in Ireland. Nell and Erin were babies and I had gone ahead to find a place. In the subway in London a fire broke out at the King's Cross station. People were running over one another to find a way out. I ran to the tracks and pushed my way inside the last car of the last train out just as the doors were closing. As the train was pulling away there were people running beside it, screaming to be let on. And when I saw the great black wall of smoke behind us, I began to speak to you.

And the flight home from Los Angeles in 1982 when the plane fell suddenly and everyone's dinner flew up to the ceiling. People were screaming but I was speaking to you as I am now.

Your bones are in the ground, seven or eight miles from where I was born, half a mile from where you last heard us cry. How far I've wandered from where you lie.

Chapter Thirty-seven

When the doctor opened Nancy Nau's belly to deliver her babies by cesarean, a hot stream of fluids shot to the ceiling like a fountain. She told me how the nurses said they'd never seen anything like that before. She began to cry when she told me that her twin girls lived only a few hours. This was in the seventh month of her preeclampsia. She said, "If your mother hadn't carried you to full term, and if I hadn't had my babies taken early, you and I wouldn't be here. Your Peggy and my twin girls died for us."

"Yes," I said.

"I'm sure your mother was beautiful and sweet and loved you and your brother so very much. Believe this, please, from someone who had the same condition as your mother. And if you want me to, I can tell you everything that your mother was going through, month by month, up to the end of her life."

"Yes," I said again.

One door opens and then another closes. I found Dr. Wright's former office nurse living now in California. When my brother and I had met him, his wife just mentioned casually that the nurse was still alive and that she called them every month or so to see how they were.

It came down to this, me walking around for five days with her name and telephone number on a scrap of paper in my pocket, too afraid to call her. Why? Because what would I do if she told me that Peggy's death was unnecessary? What if she told me that everyone who loved my mother failed her in the end; Peggy was dying in their midst and they failed to rescue her.

I had my brother call her first. She was annoyed and barely spoke to him. When I called she told me on the telephone that she had been expecting my call. "We never had a patient by your mother's name," she said.

"Maybe by her maiden name," I said.

"No one named Peggy Snyder and no one named Peggy Schwartz."

"Schwartz?" I said. "How do you know her maiden name?"

"I have to go," she said. "I'm an old woman now, and I have to go."

Chapter Thirty-eight

I know that on Mother's Day in 1950 Peggy didn't go to church because she was upset with the way her face had begun to swell. A pie face, she called it. The face of a circus freak. How could anyone expect her to believe that this was a normal part of being pregnant. Her cousin Jean was one month ahead of her in her pregnancy and she looked lovely. Her face was radiant—she had never looked prettier.

In the afternoon on Mother's Day, Peggy allowed her mother to persuade her to take a walk. Peggy wanted to carry Audrey, and she was big enough now to sort of set Audrey's bottom on her pregnant belly. They walked three blocks to East School Street where her father and Dick were working on the new house. It was a hot day and her mother brought along some lemonade in two old pickle jars with waxed paper screwed into the lids so they wouldn't leak.

Her mother was pleased to show her that the dining room was already framed. All she wanted was a dining room because there wasn't one in the half house on Market Street. Her father and Dick were so delighted to see Peggy there that they nailed together a few boards for a bench and put it in the shade of a willow tree so she and her mother and her baby sister could sit and watch them swing their hammers.

Here, on this makeshift bench, with Audrey sitting on the

ground pulling up handfuls of grass, her mother told her that she had bought a daybed for the living room. She is going to put it against the far wall, and it will be a davenport during the day and at night her bed. It won't be in the way. It won't be any trouble. She must do what the doctor has told her to do.

She takes one of Peggy's hands in hers and tells her, I don't want to argue with you or upset you, but I'm your mother and someday you'll understand the deep, instinctive desire to take care of the children God has given us.

Maybe it's not what she says that persuades Peggy. Maybe it is the sight of her father and her husband happily building the house; it makes her believe that all of them living together in the half house will work out okay. They'll be coming here straight from work each afternoon and working until it's too dark to see, and she can sit and watch them. She can watch her mother's house going up.

When Dick stops to drink his lemonade and smoke a cigarette, Peggy sits beside him in the grass. The sweat has left trails through the dirt on his cheeks. She pushes his hair back and presses the cool jar of lemonade against his forehead. The fine hair on his arms has begun to turn blond from the sun. She runs her fingers along the back of his hand and he tells her that someday he's going to build *her* a house, that her father is teaching him everything he'll need to know. And the land across the street is for sale. He has spoken with Mr. Lauchman; he's willing to arrange a loan to buy the land. Would you like this? Would this make you happy?

I'm happy right now, she says to him.

He goes on to tell her that if they move back home with her folks now like the doctor has told her to do, they can start saving money to buy things for the house he's going to build.

. . .

They are coming at her from every side. Respecting how stubborn she is and how her mind is impossible to change once she has made a decision. They are trying to appease her into agreeing to move back home.

Of all things, she tells Dick to write her a letter.

A letter?

Yes. Like the ones you used to write me after each date. Write me a letter, Dick. Tell me all about this house that you are going to build for me.

Chapter Thirty-nine

No one can tell me what became of her things that she had left in the apartment in Lansdale, expecting to return after she delivered her baby. Peggy was full of anger over losing her own place in the world, the five little rooms where she and Dick had set up housekeeping just six months earlier. The plywood cupboard below the kitchen sink where the pots and pans were kept, each of them new just half a year ago, now burned black on the bottom from when she tried to learn to cook. The hallway closet where she kept her extra shoes and the lovely married-lady dresses that she had made and then put away when she began wearing maternity clothes. Each of them on its own wood hanger covered with stiff white paper that she got from the dry cleaners.

What became of these possessions? She left behind everything that meant something to her and I will never be able to find what became of these things. I am to blame for this because for nearly thirty years of my grown-up life I never thought about her. How can I explain this? These were years when I could have found her grave on my own. Long ago I could have searched for the people who remembered her. There was nothing standing in my way. I simply forgot about her the way we do in this life. I turned and went on living.

Go and live, she might have said to me once when I was a boy. Go and live. But don't forget me.

There is Dick at the door to the apartment after Peggy walks out. He is calling to her but she just keeps marching toward the car. He is calling to her that they will be back here soon, right after the baby is born, and in the meantime he will bring anything she wants to have with her. Anything.

Just tell me what you want to take with us, Peggy.

She won't look back. She is sitting in the car with her head bowed when he carries her sewing machine down the front steps and lays it on its side in the trunk of the car.

It won't be long and we'll be back, he says as they drive away.

In her father's house they put the sewing machine in front of a window in the living room as if it is a houseplant that needs the sunlight to survive. Late at night when everyone else is sleeping Peggy stays up sewing baby clothes and Mrs. Bower takes note of this. To this neighbor there still is a logical progression in Peggy's life. She had taken note of her sewing her bridesmaids' dresses, then her honeymoon wardrobe, then the married-lady dresses, and now she has returned with her pregnant belly to sew her baby's clothes.

For the first time in her life Peggy sleeps late in the mornings. At first it takes an act of will to sleep until her husband and father have left for work. Her face and hands are most swollen in the morning and she has felt something in the way they look at her. Their fear, perhaps?

What is it that people see when they look at her? Maybe

they can tell that something isn't right with her pregnancy, and she can sense this so she hides herself away.

She hides herself away so well that all these years later I have only a mystery left in front of me, and small pieces of her secret.

But it makes sense to me. By June the shape of her face had changed dramatically, flattened without depth, and wide. So she mailed the invitations to her baby shower a week late so that no one would come. So no one would see her with her circus face.

By mid-June the severity of her illness hits her when she can no longer fit her feet into even her slippers. The toxemia that she read about in the pregnancy book has now become preeclampsia, the condition that Dr. Wright had warned her of.

Now she hides from everyone. Dick and her father work on the house until dark each day and by the time they come home she is in bed for the night. When they are asleep she goes for drives with the windows down to cool off her skin. I know that once she drove back to North Broad Street in Lansdale and parked in front of the maternity house of Elm Terrace Hospital to listen for the sound of a mother in labor. She told her cousin about this; she was right there, just across the street from her apartment, but she kept her head turned so she wouldn't have to see it.

She is becoming nocturnal by the end of June and these are strange nights. Not only are the night skies groaning with the sounds of Air Force jets from the base in Willowgrove, as many planes flying test runs now as during the war, but in Hatfield the midget race cars are speeding around the dirt track until midnight with a high-pitched grinding noise that torments her soul and vibrates her mother's china teacups. In order to drown out the maddening noise she leans her head close to the sewing machine motor as she works.

It got very bad in July. On some days she was too weak to dress. Her husband, hopeful, always hopeful, tried again and again to convince her that if she would only eat something she would start to feel better. Her empty chair at the table has come to symbolize her mother's mounting fears. She knew that something terrible was happening to her daughter. But whenever she asked Peggy if it would be all right for her to have Dr. Moyer, her childhood doctor, come by, she refused. She buried her face in her pillow and told her mother that she would be all right if only everyone would just stop talking about how terrible she looked.

She had become hideous to look at; this was the source of her greatest despair. The physical beauty that she had always placed between herself and the world had been erased, leaving her vulnerable. So vulnerable that the baby rolling inside her stomach was not a comfort or a source of amazement to her. It only made her feel like she had no place to hide.

At dusk on the days when it was quiet enough she lay on the daybed with her head on the windowsill and she could hear the sound of hammers and saws from five blocks away where Dick and her father were working on the new house. This was a comfort to her. She listened for a pattern in the sounds and pictured them working side by side. She could close her eyes and see them in their khaki pants and white T-shirts. Her mother took them their dinner wrapped in tin foil. On hot nights, a bottle of beer each. She pushed Audrey in her stroller, the tray with their picnic supper on the little metal rack below the seat. One night she was caught in a thunderstorm, great gashes of lightning in the darkening sky. When she returned she sat on the daybed and told Peggy how the lightning had struck the roof of the house, setting off sparks of electricity as it raced across the roof, skipping along the nail heads.

When Peggy spoke at all it was always about the war in Korea. That war, so far away, seemed more real to her than the possibility that soon her baby would be born and she would be delivered.

Then one night Dick awoke her with a smile on his face. He placed his hand on her stomach and told her that he'd heard from one of the fellows at work that of all the veterans on active reserve, those with children would have their names put at the bottom of the list, they would be the last soldiers called to Korea.

This was the greatest news! She propped herself up on her elbows and let him kiss her. Finally the great burden of her pregnancy made sense in a way she never could have expected.

It gave her a burst of energy. When her cousin Jean came home from the hospital with her new baby on July 23, Peggy walked up the street to see her. Jean remembers this: Her mother at the window watching Peggy walk up the sidewalk. She is moving so slowly and with such effort it is as if she is climbing a steep ladder. Jean's mother told her daughter to come to the window to watch. She told her that for a week now she hadn't seen a light at the window; Peggy had stopped sewing baby clothes and this must mean that her time was near.

She walked up the sidewalk barefoot because by now she could not fit her swollen feet in even her father's slippers.

"When I saw Peggy that day," her cousin said to me, "I almost dropped my baby."

She remembers Peggy struggling to smile. The vacant look in her eyes. Her cousin handed the baby to Peggy and thought, My God, why isn't her doctor helping her! Why isn't *someone* helping her!

Her lovely hair, which she was always so proud of, was lank, and matted against her forehead, like she'd been lost in the woods, wandering for days. Like she'd barely survived some terrible disaster. It was a hot day. Her blouse was wet with sweat.

"What can I do to help you, Peggy?" Jean asked her.

"I'm going to be all right, Jean," she replied.

Jean didn't believe this. And her unasked question—*Why isn't someone helping her?*—was left to me to answer. Swollen and misshapen, Peggy was barely able to walk; how could my father and her mother not see how terribly sick she was? How could they *not see* that they were losing her?

In Peggy's brief time on this earth she had hidden behind her beauty. But her beauty had betrayed her now, just when she needed it most, and she was left to try and hide her secret behind the nightmare that had replaced this beauty.

Her secret was that she knew she was dying. She had the memory of Dr. Wright's warning at the start of her pregnancy. His words had been only dull abstractions then, but now, in the heat of summer, she knew that her decision to take this pregnancy to the end was going to kill her.

Her beauty had betrayed her, exposing her to the questions and the fears of those people closest to her. They *did see,* of course. My father, her father, and her mother saw. I know that her mother, my grandmother, tried on several occasions to persuade her to let Dr. Moyer, their family doctor, examine her or at least come to the house on Market Street to see her. *To see what?* That some divine and grotesque trick had been played on her? He was summoned once by my father, and Peggy refused to let him into the room.

Should I blame my father for not breaking down the door?

For a week in the fall of 1998 I turned over my days and nights to this question—*Why didn't my father do something to help her?* When there was no answer, a strange anger came up in me, an anger so profound that there were times when, standing in line at the grocery store, or watching the kids play soccer, the sounds of the world fell away into silence and I was left there, talking to myself.

Finally, I drove back to Pennsylvania with this anger, pressing hard on the gas pedal all the way down from Maine as I kept imagining my father standing at my mother's grave in the weeks and months after her death. Going there by himself to speak the same question into the empty air, *Why didn't I do something to help you, Peggy?*

It was his question then, and mine when I stood at Peggy's grave the last time. Dusk had fallen and I was alone there. Leaves blew across the ground. On the wind there was a curl of dark smoke from the meatpacking plant. I bowed my head and asked for an answer. At first just with silence, and then speaking out loud, I told my mother that I would not leave until I knew why no one had come to her rescue. Cars were driving by. I was sure that I could hear them slowing down as they saw me. I tried to think back over everything that I finally knew about my mother. I was standing there a long time. Reading her name engraved in the granite marker, and then my father's, I pictured him pleading with her, and her defying him, defying everyone. I thought of her defiance, and then of her faith. And then it came to me that they were the same thing in Peggy. For what is faith but the defiance to say, *I still believe.* Despite the evidence, despite the proof, despite what everyone is telling me, *I still believe.* Despite the fear I see in my husband's eyes, and in my mother's glance, despite their warnings, I will believe that I am going to get through this. Even if it isn't true, I won't let anyone take this belief from me.

And who would dare take this from her, knowing that it was the last thing she had to hold on to, knowing, as they must have known, that it was too late for anything but a blind faith in God's love.

That is the point, really: once Peggy decided at the beginning of the summer not to end her pregnancy, there was nothing anyone could do for her but allow her the dignity of her doomed faith.

She kept it until the last day of her life when she was too weak to object and Dr. Moyer was finally summoned. As he walked into the bedroom he looked at her and the color left his face. "This is not the girl I know," he said gravely. Then he called for the ambulance.

Standing at my mother's grave that last time, I thought of my children growing up and wanting to know why the people who loved Peggy best had allowed her to die in their presence. I decided I would tell them that maybe we can't know the answer to this question until it is our turn to lose someone we love, and then we might learn that love in the end requires us to let go, to stand aside so that this person can prepare herself to fall back into the arms of the angels.

.   .   .

One day in July Aunt Lilly comes by to see her. She has a dress for Peggy that she has been working on all summer, made from a pattern that Peggy had chosen. Peggy didn't have the energy to make it herself so Lilly took over. It is a handsome gray tailored dress, and Peggy tries to thank her properly but when she holds the dress up she realizes that whoever she was before this began, she will never be that same person again. The person who might have worn this dress was lost.

Here is her aunt Lilly who had helped her sew her bridesmaids' dresses. They had spent long hours together before Peggy's wedding, and now as she stands in front of her, Peggy is trying desperately to recall what they had talked about all those nights when they were up late together sewing. If she could only remember one small thing from that lost time, just one thing, then maybe she could begin to get herself back.

Not long after Lilly's visit, Peggy decided she could no longer sleep in the living room because she was spending so much time in bed, and there was no privacy for her downstairs. And the noise that her baby sister makes is too much for her to bear when her head is aching. The bathroom is upstairs and sometimes when even the sound of people speaking below her is too much, she opens the faucet in the tub and lets the sound of running water drown out the rest of the world.

To Dick she still looked beautiful. He remembers that every day of her life she was beautiful. Up in her mother's bed he sat with her, putting cold washcloths on her head.

He tried to cheer her up. Telling her that it wouldn't be long before she and he and the baby could move back home. You're almost there, Peggy. Don't you see, you're almost there. You've been so brave through all of this. Soon now, things will return to normal. And who'll be here when you return, Peggy? Who'll be standing here waiting for you?

You will.

That's right.

Say it to me, please, Dick.

I'll be here when you return.

You will be here?

Yes, I will. Of course I will.

This was the last month she would ever see the end of. But in the final days of July she and Dick were so close that he stopped wishing away the time of her pregnancy. Instead he tried to think of each hour as a gift from God that he would appreciate fully so that he would remember. Because of her faith, his faith had never been stronger, and he was certain that God would take care of this girl he loved.

Innocent. He was innocent. She never told him anything. By the end of the month, when she got up to pee, nothing came out. She went six days without peeing a drop. All her organs were beginning to drown in the toxic fluids that ran through her. Dick granted her wish just a few days before she went into the hospital and took her back to Lansdale to see the apartment on North Broad Street. She told him how she was going to dream, through the pain of labor, of sitting on the loveseat in the front window with him and their baby between them. Sunlight falling on her baby. And playing records. She would dream that they were playing all her favorite records.

So Dick drove her back. From the street the apartment

seems already to have forgotten them, forgotten the way they had filled its rooms with love.

She begins to cry. Don't you want to go in, Peg? Dick asks her. Let me take you inside.

But she won't let him. She just keeps crying and this is the hardest thing for him to figure out; she has her faith and yet at times it seems like she has given up on everything. He will tell her once again that if she'd only start eating, she would begin to feel better. But she can tell by the flatness in his voice that he no longer believes this. He is just talking to her to try to reclaim her from the currents that are carrying her away. Does he know in some part of himself that he will never return here with her? Is he asking himself what he has done to this lovely, sad girl? What has he *not* done that he might have done to prevent this night from happening?

She didn't tell him. She didn't tell him that she was going to wander a million miles from here on another part of her journey. That she would never live here again. Never open the front door again. Never hang laundry out on the line in the backyard.

Chapter Forty

My father has told me that Peggy's faith in God was strong and that she was not afraid. He holds to this belief. Even now after I have told him the truth he never knew, he reassures me that she was not afraid.

I will believe this then, for my father's sake, and for my own. I will believe that when the first contraction came she took her deep breaths, breathing evenly and slowly, as she swung her legs out of bed. It was August 9, a Wednesday. Just before noon on a cloudless day so hot that the sidewalks burned the soles of her bare feet, she climbed behind the wheel of her father's Ford and drove herself to Elm Terrace Hospital. Even with the seat back as far as it could go, the steering wheel pressed into her stomach. Dick and her father were at work at the print shop. Her mother had gone grocery shopping, pushing Audrey along in her stroller with the fringed cloth hood blocking the sun.

Peggy had called the hospital, half an hour earlier, after a contraction took her breath away. Anna Hartman, the labor and delivery nurse, told her to come on in. There was a full moon and all but two of the beds were taken. The authority and competence in her voice was reassuring. She was calling Dr. Wright's office while Peggy was getting dressed. The only thing that fit her now was a flower-printed shift that hung off her shoulders.

Dick had packed the brown suitcase a week before. It stood next to the hot-water boiler in the kitchen and contained a comb, a brush (the matching mirror she would not let him pack), toothpaste and toothbrush, talcum powder, the pale yellow quilted gown that Lilly had sewn for her, three envelopes and sheets of paper, the pocket-sized Bible that Dick had carried with him during the war, a box of tissues, a wind-up clock, and a fountain pen and small glass bottle of ink.

The pen and ink were important because she was going to write my father letters. And he was going to write back to her, letters like the ones he wrote her after each date when they were starting out. She looked forward to this. She must have thought that as soon as her baby was delivered, she would regain her strength. No more headaches. No more blurred vision. She would be able to pee again, and she would get stronger each day in the hospital. She would finally be able to concentrate again, and to hold a thought in her mind about something other than the way her body felt.

She parked along the curb. Took her suitcase from the front seat. Who would have seen her hesitating on the sidewalk, like some weary traveler? A solitary figure with a suitcase. The same pose she had imagined her husband striking three years before, on a sidewalk in Seattle as he waited for the train that brought him home from the war, healthy and alive, so that his life could coincide with hers. Did she think of him just five blocks away now, standing at his Linotype press, the heat of the print shop gathering in his throat, causing sweat on his cheeks. He would be eating his lunch soon on the wood-planked loading dock in the alley, lighting a cigarette after he'd finished, taking a deep breath and blowing smoke into the sky. When had she stopped packing his lunch? How many weeks had passed since she last had the strength to make his lunch?

Is this the way a life runs out? Small important and unimportant things falling out of the orbit of your life because you are spinning too slowly.

This is how Mrs. Bower remembers it: Her light is on late as she works at the sewing machine. First she was making her wedding dresses, then her married-lady dresses, then maternity clothes, then her baby clothes. And then the light went out.

The light went out.

Elm Terrace Hospital's maternity wing is just a lovely old Victorian house like one of the guest houses at the Jersey shore. Canvas awnings at the front windows. Trimmed hedges. Tall elm trees. The front porch five steps up from the sidewalk.

Did she pause to glance back across the street at her brick walk-up apartment? Could she picture herself back there on that porch, or joining the parade of young mothers pushing baby carriages up North Broad Street into the future of America?

The future. Did her faith in God allow her to believe that she would claim her place among those stroller mothers taking possession of the future?

The double oak doors with their fine oval glass panels open to a foyer of dark-paneled walls and wide stairs that climb to a landing where white lace curtains are flying like sails on the summer breeze. From where she stands the stairs look so steep, just looking at them is enough to make her wonder what happened to the little girl she once was who went flying up and down the stairs at school.

A nurse called Scottie shows her to her bed. One of five in a room with brightly flowered wallpaper and white crown molding along the ceiling. More white lace curtains blowing high. Her roommates smile and say hello. None of them looks the way she looks. None has a face as badly swollen as hers.

It is her face that persuades Scottie to admit her though her contractions that morning were only false labor. Scottie writes the word *preeclampsia* above Dr. Edward Wright's name on the index card and attaches it to the rail of her bed.

Across the hallway is the nursery with fifteen cribs lined up against the walls. Beside it another room for mothers, this one with six beds. Would she remember the mothers in these other beds? The one who told her that when the moon is full, every bed is always taken and the boys from the volunteer ambulance corps who carry the mothers up to the delivery room and then back down sleep in cots on the third floor, taking catnaps between deliveries. The night nurse, Sarah Cobley, who told her to call her Sally? How she rubbed Peggy's back until she fell asleep? The coffee urn that was used to heat water in the delivery room. The kitchen stove where the glass bottles were heated.

For two days she waited for the contractions to become steady and she wouldn't eat anything. Scottie and Anna were keeping a close watch on her, aware that she might go into convulsions, knowing that in such circumstances they could lose mother and baby. Each morning when Anna arrived she checked with Sally—Has she eaten anything?

Peggy can't sleep, either. The Crying House, she calls this place. Babies always crying in the nursery, and women crying through their labor upstairs. The sound of all this crying is worse than the delirious race cars tearing around the track in Hatfield. And it's hot, it is so hot, heat from everyone's big body pushing slowly through the rooms of the Crying House. She is trapped beneath the heat and the noise and the two women in her room who call themselves veterans; they've delivered their new babies and because they have toddlers at home, they're determined to treat their ten-day recovery as a kind of vacation. Playing cards and asking for second help-ings of mashed potatoes. Eating ice cream like it is going out of style, the wrapped square slices of chocolate, vanilla, and strawberry like little flags. The same ice cream Peggy's church serves at its dinners.

Anna Hartman sits on the foot of her bed and talks with her about breast-feeding and circumcision should her baby be a boy. She uses one sheet of the paper she brought along to make Peggy a fan and as she is watching the nurse fold the paper Peggy recalls the fans that she made in grade school out of construction paper in art class along with Ginny and Adelle and Peg Kirsch. And the amazing thing is that she can see the schoolroom so clearly, the wood-and-gray-steel chairs, the water fountain in the right-hand corner across from the teacher's desk. It is all much too clearly focused to be a memory; it is part of the landscape she is passing now.

Her husband has left a letter for her, Sally reports the next morning. He stopped by on his way to work and when he found her sleeping, he left this letter with Sally.

It is just a short note telling her that he went to the apart-ment yesterday and it's very clean, just as they left it, and he didn't see any sign of the ants that she was worried about. The place is all ready for the two of them to move back home with the new baby. He doesn't want her to worry about anything because he knows that all of this was meant to be, the way they met and knew at once that they wanted to spend their lives together. And now this baby, a gift from God.

I hope she believed him. I hope she didn't lie awake in her bed, listening to the crying mothers and babies, and feeling like God had forsaken her, or was punishing her for some terrible sin. She hadn't lived long enough to pile up enough sins to justify the awful way she felt. Her mind swarming with dark thoughts, and her head aching so that it took an act of will to keep from screaming.

On the night of August 10, just before nine o'clock, Dick kissed her and told her that he would be back in the morning. She was getting very close to her time. Scottie told him that the baby would come before morning. A part of Peggy wanted him to leave so she could stop trying to conceal her pain, and another part of her wanted desperately for him to stay. If she'd had the energy, she would have begged him not to go. How wonderful it would be if someone could carry her across the street to her apartment and the doctor could deliver the baby there, in her bed, with her husband beside her.

The last thing he told her before he left was that he was going to stay up late writing her another letter, and in the morning he would bring it by for her.

She closed her eyes when he turned to leave. Scottie rubbed her back and told her that everything was going to be okay. She told her what she had told all the other mothers: "God made women to have children and you will make it through all right."

She had those words to carry her through the long night, and she had my father's promise that he would stay up late writing her a letter.

The promise was still on his lips when he left the hospital, stepping outside into the night. On the sidewalk he stood between the empty rooms of the brick apartment where he had made love to her and the lighted rooms of the hospital where this love had taken her. Love as logical as geometry.

He turned back to face the hospital which looked even more like a tourist house in moonlight, a seaside tourist house that covered the danger of what it really was. The tourists were crying in the night. Why? Because the lives they left behind when they arrived and signed in would not be the same anymore?

He couldn't drive away with her cries joining the others that night. He unlocked the apartment door. He listened to a Phillies game on the radio. He tried to fall asleep and not to fall asleep in the morris chair by the window. He kept turning down the sound on the radio, hoping that the shrieks of terror had stopped. *What have I done to her?* he thought.

Sometime in the night he did fall into his sleep as she was being carried upstairs to the delivery room by boys from the volunteer corps. Less than an hour after Dick left her with his promise to write her a letter that night, the boys from the volunteer corps who were napping on the third floor were awakened by Sally. They were as careful with Peggy as they could possibly be but still when they rounded the landing they tilted the gurney and she felt the blood rush into her head. She could hear them shuffling their feet on the wood stairs and groaning against her weight and she apologized.

Anna was plugging in the coffee urn when she was carried into the delivery room. It was just after ten o'clock. The white lace curtains hung straight down at the windows, trapped in the awful heat and humidity. "It's all right," Scottie whispered in her ear, "God made women to have babies. Everything is going to be all right now." Would Peggy try to remember this to countervail the awful smell of the black rubber mask and the nitrous oxide administered by Anna Hartman when my brother's head began to distend the muscles of her pelvis?

My mother put the lie to the wise nurse's words; everything was never all right again. At 5:30 the next morning they called my father to tell him that he had twin boys and to ask him to find someone with A-positive blood as quickly as he could. Blood types had been stamped on all GIs' dog tags, so men were familiar with theirs and my father's buddy from the print shop, Bill Crockett, was a match.

Peggy took a quart of his blood as he lay next to her on a cot. A thin tube connected her body to his. He tried to make her laugh. Her raspy laugh was one of the things Bill liked about Peggy.

No one would ever hear her laugh again. The last thing Sally did before she went off duty was call the *Lansdale Reporter* to tell them that twins had been born.

Dr. Wright only charged my father for one of the babies. Twenty-five dollars. "You're going to need to save all the money you can," he told my father. "Twins are expensive."

My father stood smiling in the doorway. It must have brought some pleasure to my mother that she had finally given him something, something no one could ever take from him. She might have pictured the three of us as friends. He would still only be in his thirties when these two boys became young men. One of us to stand on either side of him.

When he sat close to her on her bed, she said to him, "I've finally given you something, Dick."

Tears were coming down her cheeks when she told him that these two boys were for him to make up for the two brothers he had lost in his childhood. It was a miracle, really.

Last night was hard, Dick, but I still want six boys.

He remembers my mother saying this. It was proof to him that she was going to get better. And he carried it with him through the days ahead when she wouldn't eat and she grew weaker and weaker.

She was released from the hospital nine days later when the nurses could not get her to eat. She had given up by then because all along when she had been so sick during her pregnancy, my father kept telling her that all the bad stuff would go away just as soon as the baby was born, just as soon as she finally delivered the baby, and she had clung to this in order to live through those days. And then after the babies were born and she still kept feeling worse and worse, when she couldn't even begin to imagine running on her legs as she had once run on cool autumn afternoons with her field hockey team in school, before taking a job and before falling in love, before setting up her own apartment and becoming a mother, she stopped eating. She stopped trying to get better.

I keep seeing the labor and delivery nurse, Anna Hartman, standing on the porch of the hospital that morning, watching the young mother get into her husband's green Chevrolet to drive home with their newborn babies. I missed meeting Anna by two days—she died before I could talk with her. But she has been described to me as a loving, compassionate woman, someone who might have tried, for her own sake, to turn away and go back inside, but who would have lingered there on the porch to watch this ritual one more time. Wasn't this the reason that she had chosen to be a labor and delivery nurse? So she could be up close to the miracle? This ritual of a new family beginning their journey home together for the first time is always reassuring to Anna and she loves to watch, in fact she feels she must watch, must bear witness to this part of the miracle. And she always wants to say the same thing to the father and mother, to tell them that in the full cast of a life with its wide arc of possibilities, small moments like this one are often lost, and they must tell themselves never to forget how blessed they were in their youth to bring home a healthy baby. They must never forget just how insistent the promise of happiness was as they made their first trip home together.

But what kind of miracle is this, this morning when the hot sky is white with light. Anna reaches out her hand to steady herself. There are things to do inside, other mothers to attend to. She must make herself stay on the porch, she has to force herself to watch.

Anna Hartman was a wise woman and in the time she had spent with Peggy she would have ascertained that this was a rather plain girl, not a girl who would set the world on fire. She would live just an average life, sewing her boys' clothes until they wouldn't wear homemade clothing anymore, feeling the small sadness of life when these little boys who called her Mommy would one day holler behind them, "See you later, Mom," on their way out.

Always when Anna watched the new families leaving for home together, something inside her wanted to stop them and remind them to pay attention to these days. Days when they adored one another, days more precious than the treasures we dream of having in this world.

But what kind of miracle was this? This morning the promise of life seemed more tentative to Anna than ever before. She was the last person who could have stopped the young husband to tell him that his wife would not live more than a few days longer and that he should memorize her hand in his so he would never forget.

Each family driving away with a new baby is a love story. But Anna Hartman knew that my father's love story was ending. She tried not to let it touch her too deeply, but it was no use. As closely as we can feel another person's fear, she felt the fear of this young mother. The terrible fear that men never really feel the way a woman does when she asks in her sorrow, *Who will care for my children when I'm no longer here?*

Chapter Forty-one

The plan was for Peggy and Dick to take her parents' room on the second floor, but she was never strong enough to make it up the stairs, and so she resumed her place on the daybed in the dining room where, for the first two days, she wouldn't let my father out of her sight. She made him stay next to her. She was trying all over again to believe what he had told her about how everything would get back to normal now and how, before too much longer, she would move back to their brick apartment where she would be forever delivered from her dark fears and back into his hands. Delivered back into his grateful touch.

But even his presence next to her didn't end the loneliness. The loneliness inside her was now part of everything she could comprehend.

What made the days back in her father's house so difficult, what made it such a strange time, a dense and weightless, swirling time like a fever dream, was that everyone was forced to believe things that they could not imagine. Her mother, what was she to believe each of those mornings when she came downstairs from her bedroom and found the sheets on the daybed soaked in blood. How could she wash the blood off her daughter's thighs each morning without thinking about that time they went to the farm together and her daughter was enchanted by the idea of pickling and jarring so many beets that her hands would be stained red? Her mother, my grandmother, was never the same after she lost Peggy. She raised Peggy's brother and sister, then surrendered to her broken heart, spending her days feeding the cardinals that flew into her yard on School Street. She fed them through the long winters of her life, imagining at times that a certain cardinal who came back each year on Christmas morning was her daughter's soul returning to keep her company.

On those late August days she began to believe the unimaginable, that she would outlive her daughter.

And Peggy's husband, who tried to play records for her, setting up the record player in the dining room, hoping against hope that she would regain enough strength to dance one dance with him, a slow dance to the slow beating of their hearts. A rag doll in his arms. He didn't care about the dance, it was just the chance to hold her again, that's all he really wanted. What could he know for certain except the feeling deep inside that something was being taken from him now and he could not stop it from happening?

His grandmother was in the house every day to help out. She had delivered hundreds of babies and she was driving Peggy crazy, telling Peggy the same thing over and over—If you'd hold your babies, you'd start feeling better.

Peggy could hear her whispering this to everyone—If she starts holding her babies, she'll start feeling better.

Now Peggy thanked God for the midget race cars that screamed their maddening sound through town each night because they drowned out the sound of everyone whispering about her, and because if she laid her head on the windowsill, the noise from the racetrack was enough to cover the sound of her babies crying.

. . .

It came down to one last night.

It was well after midnight and on the couch across the room, my father was tossing and turning in his exhausted sleep, his feet hanging over the edge. All those times during the months when he was courting her, he would drop her off at the front door to this house and then while he was driving home, she would lie in bed wishing in the worst way that she could sleep next to him. Since she had fallen in love with him and been certain that he was the one she was waiting for, it had seemed like such a sad waste of time to her not to sleep with him. Each night was a night they would never get back. Now she wanted all of those nights back.

Tonight, outside the front window of the living room, the branches of a young birch tree waved in the warm August wind. Since coming here from the hospital, she had been aware of the smallness of her parents' house. Like the others on the block, it was divided into many rooms in an effort to give the illusion of space and privacy, but you could stand in the center of any room and stretch out your arms and nearly touch all four walls. Tonight the house seemed too small to contain her and her husband and the two babies. The house didn't seem to hold enough oxygen for everyone.

The problem with being back here under her parents' roof was that the progression in her life—the marvelous progression from being a single teenaged girl and then an engaged teenaged girl and then a married teenaged girl and then a mother—was suddenly interrupted. Here she was back home, sleeping alone again as if nothing had happened.

She gazed across the room at her husband and wished with everything in her comprehension that she felt strong enough to get up from the daybed and walk the five steps it would take to reach him. She wished she felt strong enough to get up and make him his lunch, the sandwiches that he would take to work at the print shop in the morning.

She thought how her love for him seemed to have begun in Atlantic City where he had driven her that Saturday during her seventh month of pregnancy. She stood looking at the ocean that day, wondering if the blue-green waves would be able to hold up even her great weight. Just beyond the board-walk, on the way back to the parking lot, there was an out-door shower, nothing more than a green garden hose hanging on a rusty nail inside a wooden stall, where he stopped to wash the sand off her feet so she wouldn't track it into the Chevrolet. On the way home he pulled onto the side of the road to take pictures of her and this car. It was a 1948 Chevy with grand, sweeping fenders and hubcaps that were bright disks of light. He had wanted her to stand alongside the car, a profile so he could capture her enormous belly. But she wouldn't. "A car parked next to a tank," she said. She fell asleep before they reached home, waking once and for a few seconds forgetting it wasn't a date she was on, forgetting she was married.

How this young man changed her. Something about his love for her, his way of accepting her despite her dark moods and her stubbornness, set her free to dream and to change. No one had ever heard her say that she wanted to get married young and have a family; she was headed out of town, off to a bigger, grander life. And then she met Dick, and suddenly she was a married lady who wanted to have six sons. Boys; she loved their inexhaustible energy. The way their imaginations were just beginning to take hold—explorers, sliding their canoes into the clear, cold water. They were always moving;

even when they walked they were doing a kind of dance. She liked boys emphatically, felt she understood them. They drove their cars very fast, as if they were fleeing something. They pressed girls, like their cars, to go faster, farther. She admired the way they disdained convention, defied time, challenged even the force of gravity. Boys, not girls, because a daughter might inherit all her fears, be too much like her.

She saw the fright in children's eyes—"I didn't ask to be put here!" Like her, they were not completely of this world. She suspected that little children knew the mysteries of the universe, saw the truth in things; they cried when loved ones left the room as if they thought they might never return, because sometimes in life that was what happened.

Her mother had warned her about the sadness of raising children; when they are small and eager to draw close to you, they are too young to understand you. Then when they are finally old enough to understand you, they draw away. You never really understand each other, her mother had said. Your seasons never match.

In the hospital, between her terrifying contractions, one of the nurses had said, "Boys are easier, they're not as smart and will do pretty much whatever you tell them to do." That was probably Sally, trying to get her to laugh, trying to distract her. But there was something on the nurse's face, some concern in her eyes.

When it was over, it was this nurse who held the babies up for Peggy to see, their anatomy so shockingly different from her own. Their beauty was stunning and she raised her hands at the moment she first saw my brother and me, reached for us to take us from the nurse. That was the moment the pain in her head returned, and now it was much worse than it had ever been. It felt like her skull was cracking.

· · ·

The pain had frightened her because in the misery of those last weeks of pregnancy she had allowed herself to believe my father each time he told her that once she had delivered her baby, she would begin to feel better. She would begin to reclaim herself the way the other mothers in the hospital had. Tonight as my father lay sleeping across the room, she tried to count how many days she had been at home, how many days had passed since the pain grew worse. And this frightened her, because she realized that she had been sleeping away entire days at home. She had not awakened when my father got up for work in the morning, or when he came home in the late afternoon, or when he made his bed again on the couch, or when all of them sat down in the next room for dinner and breakfast and another dinner. She had slept through her babies' crying. This thought tonight paralyzed her with fear, the same fear she had felt in April, up late in the kitchen, tearing the seams out of her maternity dresses with the feeling that an animal living secretly in the basement had found its way up the stairs and was gnawing through the door into the kitchen.

The only food that she could tolerate in her last days was the ice that my father fed her from the blue glass bowl, the blue of a mailbox. Little chips of ice that he fed her from a spoon. When she looked into his eyes as he raised the cold spoon to her lips, she could feel the world was falling away beneath her feet.

At last she called out to him that night, called his name softly and tried to move toward him. It was another hot and humid night and he slept with his shirt off, his wire-rimmed glasses folded on the mantel. Her legs were as heavy as iron to move, swollen twice their size as if they'd been blown up with a tire pump. And there he was, so thin, growing thinner every day now, seeming to get thinner right before her eyes whenever she answered the question that he kept asking her—Are you still bleeding, Peggy?

It was his fear that seemed to diminish his size.

The same fear was in her mother's eyes when she changed the sheets. The look in her eyes that cried out—For God's sake, Peggy, how can you have any blood left!

She wanted to wake her husband now, to bring him into the daybed, to tell him her terrible, terrible thoughts. But she was distracted then by a noise in the kitchen, the rattling of glass bottles in the pot of boiling water on the stove. She wondered angrily how she had slept through this sound! Then the sound of her mother's slippers on the linoleum floor. She wished that her father had gotten up for this feeding. There was something she wanted to talk with him about. Ever since her pregnancy had begun to show, he seemed to be backing away from her, keeping his distance. She thought back to the nights when she had stood outside with him as he watched the skies. The war was on, and he was always watching for enemy planes overhead. He stood in the grass, his suspenders buckling a little each time he tipped his shoulders back to look up at the sky.

But then, with her pregnancy, he began backing away. Maybe he was just stepping aside because he knew that she would be too busy to have much time for him anymore. She would leave him.

Tonight she felt guilty for taking over her father's tiny house this way. The cot in the living room, things for the babies piled on every chair. Even the familiar scent of his aftershave lotion and her mother's baking had given way to tonics, powders, disinfectants, and diapers. She was taking over his tidy house, making a mess of it.

His radio was pushed into a corner behind a chair. She remembered the day her father brought the big radio home, setting it carefully in the living room as if he were putting a monument in place. Its resonance in this house, its lighted blue dial, its doors like the doors of the Lutheran church in town. And when he fixed up the basement and brought home their first washing machine. Once she had roller-skated off the landing and fallen down the stairs to the basement floor, landing on her wheels and rolling along as if nothing had happened. Until now she had always felt safe in her father's house.

More than anything else, she wanted to feel safe again. She wanted to get up and hold these people she loved, and make the most of this time they had together because she knew that no matter how hard these days were, these were the days they would all look back on, wanting to have them back again.

Soon her mother was standing at her side, apologizing. But Peggy began yelling at her. They're my babies, I want to feed them. They're not yours, they're mine!

Her mother's hands were open at her sides, pleading with her. You need to rest, you need to save your strength.

And then it returned—the pain like a cold spark exploding in the back of her head. Her voice woke my father. On the clock it was 1:30.

When the babies began crying to be fed, the milk ran from her nipples.

My father had brought the record player from the apartment because Peggy told him that as soon as she got out of the hospital she was going to start dancing herself back into shape. She was determined to regain her figure, and to remain a girl, always a girl. She would still go barefoot, babies or no babies, and she would keep her hair long, the curls hanging in her face. She would resist growing up for as long as possible, and then yield an inch at a time.

She heard her mother's voice but it seemed to be coming from far, far away. She kept dreaming about the little brick apartment, she kept moving the furniture around in her mind, trying to figure out if there would be room for two cribs. Two babies! It was a wonder. Down the hallway they were stirring. The two of them in one crib, sleeping horizontally, one at each end. She pictured them: little oblongs of heat and light; hair like corn silk.

I'm only nineteen, she said to her mother. I just need a little time to get used to them.

Her mother held up two little sailor outfits—cloth coats, matching short pants, and kneesocks—as small as dolls' clothes.

Please, Peggy told her, don't let them cry. The sound of them made the blood rush to her head.

She looked past her mother, back to my father asleep on the couch. She felt his loneliness. He didn't really even know her, know who she was. The two of them hadn't had enough time, they hadn't eaten enough meals together, just the two of them across the narrow tin table in their own apartment. His gestures were still unfamiliar to her. She looked at him asleep on the couch, studying him, trying to memorize him.

It was strange, but when she turned her head and looked back at her mother, she thought for a moment that they were all on the farm in Hatfield, the farm where her mother had lived as a girl.

Outside on the clothesline, the diapers were white squares in the moonlight, like bandages.

They're good boys, aren't they? she asked her mother. She

already pictured us running. Someday she would tell us about Jim Thorpe, the American Indian boy who ran like the wind. She told her mother how she was going to move all the furniture in the apartment so there would be room to push us around in our stroller, *inside.*

Inside? her mother asked.

I don't want to take any chances with polio, she explained. Visitors would have to stare at her babies through the glass windows of the apartment. Her idea was to protect us within a cocoon of love. During the war, when she had stood outside on the lawn watching the sky with her father, her own life had seemed far off, beyond the stars. But somehow she had found her way, everything had come to pass exactly as she'd hoped it would. Now the love for my father—her husband—and for the babies was self-contained, prepossessing. She was too sick to hold us, but she wanted us nonetheless. We were all encased within her love for us, a love that would immure us from the world's sadness, from all loss and longing.

When the cold spark of pain exploded again in her head she asked her mother to wake her father. He came down the stairs, trying to put his glasses on. Then she asked him to carry her up to their bed.

My father awoke then as she was being carried away. If only she had had the strength to explain to him why she wanted to spend the last night of her life away from him. They were young, their marriage so new, and their love for each other so strong that she knew his heart might try to follow hers into the next world. She had to do something to make him relinquish her. She had to push him away so he wouldn't follow her. So he would stay and take care of her babies. How my father's heart had been set upon going with her.

. . . .

Five years after her death my father drove us and a pretty girl to Atlantic City for a day on the beach. There was a strong undertow, I remember. We drank orange soda in thick glass bottles. It was the first time in my life I got water up my nose and in my ears. My father showed me how to tilt my head and jump up and down on one leg. By now there was someone new in his life. For a while I thought she was my sister. "Call her Ruthie," he had told me. "Daddy's Ruthie." She had been working in an office at the American Tile Company in Lansdale, typing through her tears the afternoon she heard of the death of a nineteen-year-old mother of newborn twins. *The poor family,* she thought. *The poor husband.* She closed her eyes and said a small prayer for him, not knowing that she would one day take my father by the hand and, in her unconditional love for him, help him face the world again, *his world* which had changed forever and yet still held starlight and the warmth of spring.

She made the picnic lunch that day at the beach. When it was time to leave, she must have walked on ahead while my father stopped at the outdoor shower to wash the sand off my feet. I remember a garden hose was hanging from a nail inside the wooden stall. After I was finished, as my father took off his shirt to step under the hose, his wallet fell from his pocket and a photograph dropped to the ground. The black-and-white picture of his young pregnant wife, sitting at the open window of the new Chevy. The sweeping fenders, the hubcaps bright disks of light.

I looked into my father's eyes and asked him who she was. I was frightened by the photograph because I had seen her before, in my bedroom when she came gliding in through the window, her face atop a column of white light, calling for me by my first and middle names. So I told him that I had seen her, and he looked at me and then washed the sand off my feet with the hose.

He waited a few more years, and then he told me that she had been my mother.

My grandfather told me how she had asked him to carry her upstairs so she could spend that last night beside her mother. She was frightened, and all night she trembled. In the first light of morning she asked her mother to bring the babies to her. She told her mother that she wanted to smell us. We were sleeping when she held us to her face and she kissed our eyelids.

In the hospital my father was down the hallway calling all his friends from high school, asking them to come to the hospital to give blood. He returned to her room once and told her that she had nothing to worry about because he was going to call Jack Graham, the tall, strong tackle from the old high school football team and with Jack Graham's blood in her she would be fine.

My father smiled at her as he left the room. A moment later she cried out, "My head, my head." She raised her hands up into the air and that was all. Through his tears, her father told the nurse that he had helped bring her into this world and now was sending her on. She took the wedding ring off Peggy's finger and placed it in his hand.

Chapter Forty-two

On the night of August 14, 1998, I dreamed that I was with my mother. My brother and I were babies again and Peggy was carrying us in her arms. She was happy and strong and we were pressed against her. As she walked along, people stopped her to say hello and to tell her how beautiful her little twin boys were, and then suddenly there was a flash of bright light and we all disappeared. It was a dream so vivid and real that with the flash of light I awoke, and I could not fall back to sleep.

In the morning on the news there was a report of another bombing in Northern Ireland. Not many details were given at first but for some reason I was drawn to the story. I was building a bench in my shop and I kept the radio on all day, listening for more information. Just before dinner I heard that among the twenty-eight people killed in the blast was a mother with twins in her belly two weeks from birth.

No matter how I tried, I couldn't stop thinking about this. Two days later I flew to Belfast and took a train to the small city of Omagh where the bomb had exploded.

From the moment I arrived, I was struck by the silence of the city. The only sound in the streets was the rain striking the plastic wrapping of the thousands of flower wreaths and bouquets that leaned against the storefronts down the length of the high street from the courthouse, along Market Street, around the corner of the old Dublin Road and across the Drumagh Bridge. There were also hundreds of candles sputtering in the cold wind and the rain. People stopped to pour the rainwater off those that had gone out, then knelt down on the wet bricks and relit them.

My first morning there I found my way to the little farming village of Augher where I walked a narrow road to Saint McCartin's church for two miles through the deep green hills of the Clogher valley, past tin-roofed barns, grazing tan sheep, and cows with noses shining from the wet grass. The little calves ran in fear to their mother's side when I passed by on foot. Inside the ancient black stone walls of the churchyard there was the new grave. Flowers in the shape of teddy bears. Plastic bottles of holy water. Little statues of the Blessed Mother and the pope.

While I was sitting at Avril Monaghan's grave, the sky darkened and it began to rain. It turned to a downpour and then stopped as suddenly as it had begun, and as the sky brightened, I knew why my father had never spoken to me and my brother about Peggy. He had to make himself *not remember* his love story in order to love his sons. If he was to become the great father he turned out to be, a father who was always for his boys, he had to forget that these boys had killed the girl he loved. It was this, or each time he looked at us he would have hated us more.

When I visit him again to tell him this, he is cold and wears a sweater though the temperature is in the nineties. He says a prayer that we will all be together someday and I am thinking about how weary Peggy must have been in the August heat that summer long ago. How do you tell the world that you just can't take another step?

It was two weeks before my father could return to work. The first thing he did was go to the man who owned the print shop and try to give back his paycheck. I didn't earn this, he said to Mr. Lauchman.

Mr. Lauchman told him to keep it. As long as I'm the boss around here, I'll decide who gets paid. All right? Good, now take care of yourself, Dick. You're going to need things for those boys of yours, so I want you to come to me, I want you to get in the habit of coming to me for help.

There were tears in his eyes when he said this.

Before the end of August 1950, my father was notified that his active reserve status had changed, and he was to prepare to go with the army to Korea. But my grandfather appealed on his behalf at the draft board in Philadelphia and my father was granted a hardship discharge. Peggy's death spared him from that war which she was so afraid would take him away from her.

A great sorrow fell over Hatfield, Pennsylvania, when my mother died. I can imagine her great difficulty in the end when her soul was ready to go home but the rest of her wanted to stay and live on. Her soul had traveled years to get here, but I think she was always moving in the wrong direction. Her melancholy, as much a divine and solemn part of her as her heart or lungs, prevented her from being completely in this world. Her soul was always leaning toward its home.

But in the end it still must have been hard for her. The body recalls such wonderful moments and wants to stay. Her legs recalled pumping hard on her first bicycle. Her arms remembered her husband's embrace.

In the end he couldn't grant her last wish. She begged him not to let them take her to the hospital. She wanted to stay home. When he told her that there was no choice, she asked him to let her ride with him in his car, no ambulance. Even this he couldn't grant her. But he promised her that he would bring her back home before the end of the day. Home before dark, he promised.

The one blessing was that he didn't have to tell us that our mother had died. This wasn't a small thing for which he was grateful; it was a very big thing for which he thanked God in heaven. It seemed like a blessing and he was thankful, always thankful. How awful if we had been older, four, five, or six. He would have had to take us in his arms and explain that the mother we had depended upon and loved was never coming home again. That, he would never have been able to bear.

But I think too that if we had been older, if my brother and I had lived in our mother's presence long enough to absorb her, then my father would have been consoled by this throughout his life—each time he ached for her he could have held one of us, or put his arm around one of us, maybe even spoken to us about her, about some moment recalled so vividly that he might forget for a moment that she was never coming back. Two sons to console him. As it was, when he lost Peggy, he lost everything and he fell to his knees beneath a sorrow as wide as the world.

The last time I saw my father he took my arm and led me to the table in front of the couch. "Sit down," he said, "I have something to look at with you."

It was the wedding album.

We sat there for a long time. Before I left I shared with him the words I had written to my mother when I was in

Northern Ireland, sitting at the new grave of Avril Monaghan and her babies.

Away from ourselves, Peggy—this is how we move through life. How far we all go away from ourselves, before we return. Such a long way back the soul must travel through the deep silence of light and shadow. Reversing every mile. Retracing each step. In the hospital when all the visitors had gone, and it was only you there with these babies that were already trying to possess you, could you feel your own beginning in theirs? Counting fingers and toes as your mother once counted yours. In the smallness, the impossible smallness of these babies, was the path made clear to you? The path back through stars and memory that your husband will travel one day to meet you. A lighted way across the oceans of time that your sons, my brother and I, will one day take home to be with you.

Acknowledgments

Lynn Nesbit and Victoria Wilson brought this book into the world. James Robinson and Jim Wright, dear old friends, were the first to help me believe that I could write Peggy's story, and Colin Harrison persuaded me that it was my duty to write it. Ruth Cramer gave my father hope and filled my mother's absence with love and compassion. James Sullivan took time away from his novel to show me how to structure this book. Colleen and our children, Erin, Nell, Jack, and Cara, gave me my own love story. Johnny Guarino talked with me on the night of September 20, 1997, when my mother's angel visited me in South Hadley, Massachusetts.

I thank them all.

And the many others who supported me: Jack and Roberta Schwartz, Eric Beesemyer, Liz Luisi, Kathleen Kennedy, Katie Long, Edgar A. Beem, Tony Anaman, Bryce Roberts, Bill and Linda LeBlond, Muriel Schwartz, David Schwartz, Robert and Linda Girardi, Paul Mooney, John Hubbard, Callie Curtis, John and Cecelia McQuinn, Ruth Wack, Tom Pugles, Jack Graham, Jean Husted, Ruth Bickhart, Adelle Bedrossian, Peg Kirsch, Anna Harvey, Bill Wack, Julia Kulp, Amber Hartman, Jenny Collins, Lorraine London, Nancy Nau, Evelyn Kinsey, John Woodcock, Naomi Myers, Jere Doherty, John Bradford, Richard Kreible, Pat O'Donnell,

Jason Kaufman, Doug Eisenhart, Eric Guckain, Burt Throckmorton, Wes McNair, Melissa Falcon, David Scheier, Tom Grimes, Jesse Workman, James and Kerri White, Audrey Corby, Shaun Sullivan, Ted Eldrege, and my twin brother, David, who took this journey with me.

Permissions Acknowledgments

Colleen Snyder

ABOUT THE AUTHOR

DON. J. SNYDER lives in Maine with his wife and their four children. He is the author of a memoir, *The Cliff Walk*, a biography, *A Soldier's Disgrace*, and three novels, *From the Point*, *Veteran's Park*, and *Night Crossing*. His new novel, *Fallen Angel*, will be published in December.